WE ARE *all* WITCHES

WE ARE *all* WITCHES

How Ancient Magic Lives in Our
Everyday Rituals and Traditions

By

Lida Pavlova

MIAMI

Copyright © 2026 by Lida Pavlova.

Published by Key Lime Publishing, a division of Media Agency Services (MAS) LLC.

Cover Design: Ivan Sennikov & Megan Werner

Cover Illustration: dikifajarfadilah, Fefelova Yana, New Africa, Yan, ⋆ Bizarre Factory ⋆ / adobe.stock.com

Layout & Design: Megan Werner

No part of this book may be reproduced, stored in a retrieval system, or transmitted in any form or by any means—electronic, mechanical, photocopying, recording, or otherwise—without the prior written permission of the publisher, except in the case of brief quotations embodied in critical articles or reviews.

Key Lime Publishing supports authors' rights to free expression and artistic creativity. Copyright exists to encourage the creation of original works that enrich our culture and society. We ask readers to respect the intellectual property of our authors and to honor their work as you would your own.

For permission requests, please contact the publisher at:
Key Lime Publishing
5966 South Dixie Highway, Suite 300
Miami, FL 33143
info@keylimepublishing.com

For special orders, quantity sales, course adoptions and corporate sales, please email the publisher at orders@keylimepublishing. For trade and wholesale sales, please contact Ingram Publisher Services at
customer.service@ingramcontent.com or +1.800.509.4887.

We Are All Witches: How Ancient Magic Lives in Our Everyday Rituals and Traditions

Library of Congress Cataloging-in-Publication Number: Requested
ISBN: (pb) 978-1-68481-881-5 (e) 978-1-68481-882-2
BISAC category code: OCC026000 BODY, MIND & SPIRIT / Witchcraft

Printed in the United States of America

Table of Contents

Foreword — 6

Introduction: The Magic Hiding in Plain Sight — 8

Chapter 1: Are We All Doing Witchcraft? Yes and No — 17

Chapter 2: What Do We Call Witchcraft? — 28

Chapter 3: The Human Mind in Search of Meaning and Mystery — 44

Chapter 4: Seasonal Rituals — 57

Chapter 5: Household Magic — 95

Chapter 6: Magical Food — 127

Chapter 7: Protection Spells (Even Those We're Barely Noticing) — 147

Chapter 8: Rites of Passage — 159

Chapter 9: We Are All Oracles — 184

Chapter 10: Momentary Magic — 200

Conclusion: Living a Life Lit with Magic—Whether You Believe or Not — 213

Further Reading — 220

Acknowledgments — 222

About the Author — 223

Foreword

I first stumbled upon Lida the same way many modern witches find each other these days: through social media. Her work radiates an ancient wisdom that feels as though it's been delivered by our ancestors themselves. Cognizance and insight can be found in every piece of content she shares; it was this, along with the energy her content exudes, that made following her a natural act of intuition. Even now, I find myself anticipating every new post.

And each time, I'm never disappointed. Everything she shares is a fragment of ancient knowledge resurfacing. When I found out she was going to write a book, I knew it would be something authentically magickal. I could not wait to get my hands on it! But even with all my excitement, nothing prepared me for what I was about to read. Lida handed me a timeless grimoire that has survived countless generations of witches: a collection of long-forgotten secrets of nature, knowledge, and intuition. This book doesn't just inform us about magick; it *remembers* it. It shows us that magick isn't something we acquire. It's something we inherit without realising it. It's always been flowing through our blood. Our role is simply to tap into it.

Through the rituals passed down in our families, the superstitions we follow without doubt, and the ways we celebrate the seasons, Lida reveals what we've always known deep down: there has always been magick in our hearts. Magick moves through us daily, whether we acknowledge it or not.

She covers folklore, ancestral magick, and personal reflection; each page feels both enlightening and comforting. Reading this book is like sitting down with a wise old friend who opens a door you didn't realise existed: where the ordinary becomes sacred and the mundane becomes ritual. Coincidences turn into messages and signs. Everyday life becomes a tapestry of magickal awareness waiting to be noticed.

What I love most is that this book doesn't ask you to be a witch. It simply shows you that, in many ways, you already are. It reminds you of the instincts you've inherited, the quiet inner knowing you've ignored, the timeless part of you that still listens for signs, honours cycles, and feels the unseen. It reconnects you to the magick that has always been quietly guiding your steps, even when you believed you were walking alone.

In a time when so much of our spiritual connection happens through screens and can often be easily forgotten, I'm grateful for *We Are All Witches*. It reminds us that the spells we cast now are the same ones cast by those who walked before us, carried from generation to generation. This is more than a book; it is a gentle reminder of where you came from, an awakening to where it all started.

I am honoured to introduce Lida's work to you, not just as someone who shares her passion for the craft, but as someone who has been continuously moved by her wisdom and presence. What you're about to read will guide you through the journey into the hidden magick that has always lived inside of you.

—*Lilly Statham*
(Mysticprimrose)

Introduction

The Magic Hiding in Plain Sight

Long before the calendar gave us tidy holidays with store-bought symbols, people marked the turning of seasons with music, food, fire, and, often, laughter. In parts of ancient Europe, the first plowing of spring was a ritual affair. The village gathered, fields still wet and shining with thaw, and the first furrow was turned with a mixture of reverence and raucous joy. Lewd jokes were told, songs were bawdy, and couples might roll together in the newly broken soil. It was no accident. The earth was being awakened, fertilized, actively encouraged. And laughter, like newly planted seeds, was seen as something that could grow.

Centuries later, a curious tradition flowered in medieval churches: the *risus paschalis*, or "Easter laughter." On the Sunday of the resurrection, priests and preachers would deliver not only sermons but jokes, from gentle puns to earthy tales, to make the congregation laugh aloud. The joy of Christ's victory over death had to be embodied, even in chuckles and snorts. Some claimed it was a way to "trick the devil," who thought he had won. Laughter, again, was holy mischief.

We carry an echo of this spring laughter ritual in the misrule of April Fools' Day. Jokes and trickery, light embarrassment, and wild reversals—all in the brief season between winter's grip and spring's full bloom. Underneath the comedy, something older: joy as a ritual, a spell, a symbolic seed. Fun as something that actually gives life. And when is that fun most needed? In spring, of course, when nature needs to awaken and prepare to bear new fruit. And we humans have to help it.

Without realizing it, you might be practicing the same old rites, softened by time and stripped of their sacred names, but pulsing with meaning. Habits and traditions are often echoes of ancient magic: rituals so deeply rooted that they've disguised themselves as common sense or just a bit of fun.

Everyday Magic Around the World

We all grow up surrounded by tiny rituals and small spells we barely notice—so normal and mundane they seem to us. Some of these rituals are widely known all over the globe. Mothers sing lullabies with verses about protection and the well-being of their children. A popular tradition from Russia (where I grew up) is divination on a chamomile flower. It is widely believed that you can find out a person's feelings for you by plucking the petals in sync with the poem "Loves, doesn't love, will spit on you, will kiss you, will hold you to their bosom, will send you to the devil." The last petal left to pluck tells you when to stop: The line you've stopped on is your result. This mirrors the "He loves me, he loves me not" petal-pulling practice popular in Western Europe and the US. People gather together to celebrate festivals with different names, but that all happen around the solstices and equinoxes...

Some of the rituals are local: widespread in certain countries but never heard of in others. For example, in Slavic countries, if you see a ladybug, you gently hold it on your finger and say:

*"Ladybug, go fly to the sky,
Bring us good bread, both black and white."*

Then you blow on the ladybug, lightly. As it flies away, you are sure that it's going to bring you luck and prosperity. Kids count crows or magpies and make predictions based on the result.

These are just two examples of local magic that are so common in some parts of the world that even little kids perform the simple rituals. Such things aren't considered witchcraft or sorcery. They are just tradition: but what is tradition if not ancient knowledge and practice passed down through generations?

There are also unique kinds of rituals honored in particular families. It might seem to us that they are just something we came up with: our own personal traditions, both fun and meaningful. But if we look closer, we'll see the common roots of the same old magic—for some reason, some seeds of ancient practices choose to grow in one particular family, and others take root elsewhere...

These practices can look very personal—and even silly—but still hold resemblance to the core principles of magic, if we examine them closely. When I was little, my mother and I enjoyed a specific kind of animal-shaped cookie. They weren't especially tasty: just dry, boring pastry. But we loved them for their shapes: cows, dogs, giraffes, ducks, pigs, horses—all mixed together. We used to put the cookies in a big bowl, close our eyes, and pull out a cookie at random. Each animal came to have a meaning: a pig predicted a good meal, a dog meant fun and good times, a duck signified rest and me-time (because we saw her as taking a relaxing bath). This was just a piece of family fun, but it also holds a striking resemblance to old divination practices, even with ancient Roman haruspicy, where sacred animals' entrails were pulled out at random and "read" as omens.

Magic in Modern Life

While you were growing up, you probably heard a lot of superstitions. Knock on wood if you don't want to jinx your luck. Don't sit at the corner of the table or you'll never marry. Cross the street to avoid black cats or bad luck will follow you.

You might have dismissed it as "old folks' talk"...but the truth is, many of us find ourselves doing just the same things our grandparents did. If you pay some attention, you start seeing that even the least superstitious, most skeptical, and extremely modern-minded people can't help but do a little witchcraft here and there. Placing family photographs (or even urns) on a mantelpiece? Echoes of cults of the ancestors, connected with hearths long before people started living in houses. Blowing out candles on a birthday cake? Ancient fire magic, done on a day we now consider a milestone and a time of transition. Giving gifts to your friends, family, and neighbors on winter holidays? Just the thing our pagan ancestors did on the night of the winter solstice. Retelling a weird dream you had last night and trying to figure out what in the world it could mean? Dream interpretation was a daily ritual in many communities all over the world.

You can't help doing something magical! But why are we like that? And, even more importantly, does this work? Is it still magic or just a bunch of habits, just the way we were taught to act? Have these countless ancient rituals survived to guide and help us through time, or are they completely powerless in the modern age?

Of course, the answer depends on who we ask. Some people try to deny and eradicate magic. They fight fiercely against the old superstitions—often creating new ones to replace them with.

Most people don't dwell on such matters but carry on actively participating in all those small magical things. Some magical traditions hold a lot of fun: gathering around the fire on Mayday with friends, exchanging gifts, keeping a lucky coin in your wallet... Why would you want to stop? Other rituals feel really sensible: Of course we should honor the dead and behave properly in the process! Of course we should clean our homes in spring! Of course it's a good idea to name a child after their grandparent or great-grandparent! It's just common sense, isn't it?

Investigating the Living Past

But there are many curious minds out there who genuinely love all things magical. For those people (among whom I count myself), it is a great thrill to find out that a mundane thing we do without a second thought has, in fact, ancient roots so deep we touch prehistory through them.

I've always been highly interested in why my relatives or acquaintances do certain "quirky" things. It got even more fascinating when I discovered that there was no logical explanation for them. That meant some kind of magic was at work, something ancient and mysterious, and it was up to me to figure out exactly what.

I grew up in Russia, later lived in various places across the Balkans, and now live in Serbia. Naturally, Slavic culture has always surrounded me, and I'll be using examples from those traditions, which I know firsthand. At the same time, I've studied many European traditions and cultures (and I've been lucky that the city I live in now, Belgrade, was once home to the ancient Celts, who called it *Singidunum*). European magic and customs will therefore make up a significant part of this book. I am less familiar with, for instance, the Indigenous cultures of the Americas, but I can confidently trace how magical rituals and traditions from Europe were "transported" to the American continent and evolved there: sometimes in parallel with Europe, sometimes in completely unique ways.

Delving into folklore and folk practices, I see how similar the fundamental principles of human spiritual thinking are everywhere and, by extension, so are the laws of magic. Yes, each culture has developed astonishing, distinctive, and unique details on top of this foundation, but most of the time, modern "everyday rituals" rest on that same ancient and basic logic.

When I was studying at university, my professor of prehistoric art used to say that noticing differences and unique traits is important, but it's meaningless until we also see the similarities and shared foundations between different cultures, eras, or objects. That's why the first thing to focus on is those commonalities. I will rely heavily on this principle as I draw my parallels between ancient and contemporary magic.

Magic Connects Us with the Past—But Does It Work?

This sacred and living thread ties our ancestors to our own habits and ways. It holds wonder and mystery, and even a sprinkle of spookiness when we start seeing that basically half of the little habits we do daily are nothing less than thousands-of-years-old witchcraft and sorcery.

Does such magic still work? Does it still hold any power or did it expire centuries ago, leaving just an empty shell of habit behind? You'll find many answers to these questions in the pages that follow.

Some would say that it didn't work before and doesn't work now; it's a bunch of superstitions and misconceptions. But if that's so, why are we still doing it? Because it's fun? But not all of the old rituals found in modern-day life are fun—some are solemn and even ominous, like funeral rites. Maybe we still do these things because we are superstitious and irrational. This answer seems to be closer to the truth, but we'll have to explore further in this book whether it is a good or a bad thing.

There are, of course, quite a lot of people who find value in traditions and customs, even if they are unsure or completely unaware of the origins of these omnipresent magical acts. Old magic is still magic (and, maybe, even more so). What worked for our ancestors will probably work for us, too.

The Power of Tradition

I believe the rituals done habitually and with our everyday surely are the strongest. Widely practiced witchcraft can be more efficient than practices only continued by a few—even if the practitioners wouldn't think about calling it witchcraft.

When I talk about "power," in this book, I mean a lot of things. The potential to transform our lives, to change the way we live day by day, year by year. The ability to form a link between our subconscious minds and our consciousnesses, and to nourish these connections with sweet irrationality. And yes, I deeply believe we, as humans, need irrationality. It is healing and wholesome to our psyches. For some reason, we are never quite satisfied with only the facts we know for sure. The mystery, for most of us, persists in the mundane, but it works and feeds us its subtle magic from there.

Seeing the Magic in Everyday Life

That's why I believe we all can benefit from a deeper look into the old traditions which live side by side with us, right here and now. When we start to consciously notice the sacred fabric of our daily lives, this magic brightens up. This feels like alchemy: connecting rational understanding of the historical roots behind the living tradition with purely irrational, childlike wonder and joy of suddenly finding a shiny mystery, hidden in plain sight.

Our Magical Quest

So, let's start this journey! We'll look into different areas of simple human experience in search of forgotten magic. We'll explore seasonal celebrations to marvel at their antiquity and original meanings. We'll walk around our homes, ready to find ghosts, helpful entities, and ancestral spirits there. We'll examine the foods we've loved since childhood and taste the spells and blessings in them. We'll go through our cupboards and cabinets to find protection talismans in simple things we use without a second thought. We'll visit special occasions and celebrations known to all of us: weddings and birthday parties, baby showers and funerals. Do you think we'll find some magic there as well?

And, finally, we'll see magic in our own selves. We've all been oracles and predicted something during our lives. We've all practiced wish-making, and manifested things into being... Whether you believe me or not, I invite you to come with me on this adventure and find out for yourself.

Chapter 1

Are We *all* Doing Witchcraft? Yes and No

Exploring the fine line between tradition, superstition, and modern-day enchantment.

Witchcraft is often imagined as something distant, fantastical, or even forbidden—a secret knowledge practiced only by the bold or the outcast. And yet, the threads of magic run through our everyday lives. In this chapter, we will explore those subtle, overlooked currents: the small acts, habits, and traditions that have survived centuries of change, sometimes stripped of their original meaning, sometimes still carrying a spark of the ancient world.

We'll look at the thin line between intention and habit, between superstition and ritual, and between the familiar and the magical. From decorative plates to lucky charms, from funeral customs to water offerings, these practices remind us that humans have always sought protection, connection with the unseen, and a little guidance through the randomness of life. By tracing these fragments of magic, we begin to see a pattern: witchcraft is not some label for certain people or certain acts—it is a living, breathing aspect of culture, memory, and belief.

This chapter invites you to notice, reflect on, and even experiment with the quiet magic that surrounds you. You don't need to call yourself a witch or even fully believe it. What matters is recognizing the continuity between ancient ways and modern life and understanding how the same impulses that gave rise to spells, charms, and rituals still shape us today. In short, we will uncover how much of what we do—intentionally or not—echoes the practices of our distant ancestors and why that matters for how we live and perceive the world now.

The Question of Intention

A common theme among modern practicing witches is that it's the intention that matters. Strictly speaking, you can't do a spell without deciding that it's a spell and without scripting (on paper or in your mind) the desired outcome or effect. If you light your candle with an intention to manifest something, then you're casting a spell, of a sort. If you're simply lighting a candle, it's just a candle: nothing witchy about it. From this perspective, we can be sure: we aren't doing witchcraft unless we are here to do some witchcraft.

Moreover, we even might be up to some magic, try to manifest some little miracle, or expect spiritual help—but not see it as witchcraft. In this case, we aren't doing witchcraft either: everyone is free to define their practices and beliefs. We'll dive into the definitions and concepts in the next chapter. For now, it's enough to say that unless you explicitly define what you're doing as such, you're not practicing witchcraft.

Distant Cousins of Magic

The more accurate way to think about that would be: What if we all do certain things that stem from the same root as witchcraft does? What if our habits and traditions were supposed to be magical hundreds and thousands of years ago? What if modern witchcraft and our mundane traditions are related to each other as siblings, or, at the very least, as distant cousins? And wouldn't it be interesting to meet their common ancestor—ancient magical and spiritual practices and beliefs?

Tradition with Forgotten Meaning

Let me give an example: a plate with a decorative rim. Pottery with rim decoration was in use among people starting from the Neolithic period (roughly the seventieth to fortieth centuries BCE). The rim, among other things, served a protective (apotropaic) function. This pattern formed a kind of protective circle, not letting evil spirits into the vessel (and into foods and drinks). Nowadays, a rim is still a popular decorative element on any kind of plate, platter, bowl, teacup, etc. We don't choose it for that ancient protective function. We simply think it's harmonious, classic, traditional, or simply looks good and familiar. In this case, the original magic of the tradition is completely forgotten by a common user, but the tradition itself persists.

In this case, it is appropriate to talk about tradition: something we do or have in our lives, but don't give much thought. Why? "It's always been this way" or "It seems natural" or "That's just something people do, right?" Its origins are ancient, its meaning was magical from the beginning, and now we still do things in a certain way, but all the magic of it is lost on us.

> *Small Spell to Find the Magic You're Already Doing*
>
> Think about something you do from time to time that feels at least a little bit irrational or has some extra meaning for you personally. Maybe you always stir your drink clockwise or say hi in your mind to a tree you pass by on your way home…
>
> Think about this personal tradition and try to define the feelings it brings you; try to understand its meaning for you.
>
> Next time you do this, take time to stop for a moment and say to yourself:
>
> "This time, it is a spell."

Magic We Half-Believe In

One of the oldest and most widespread traditions around the world is throwing coins in water. Water bodies were considered places of residence for water spirits, as well as the gateways to spiritual realms in general. Long before coins were used, people left offerings at sacred springs, wells, lakes, and other water bodies. They sacrificed food, weapons and tools, jewelry, idols or figurines...and, unfortunately, sometimes even animals and humans.

Nowadays, throwing a coin in a well, spring, lake, sea, or any other body of water is still widely practiced in many parts of the world. The most famous modern example would probably be the Trevi Fountain in Rome. Throwing a coin over your shoulder into the fountain supposedly guarantees your return to Rome (it actually worked for me once).

In Scotland and Wales, coins are thrown into certain holy wells for luck and healing.

In pre-Soviet Russia, throwing coins into wells and springs could be done with different purposes: you could basically either bless or curse anyone you wanted for a small donation to the water spirits. This practice has transformed with time: in Soviet Russia, people throw coins in fountains, springs, or the sea to ensure they return there one day or for good luck. There is also a custom in Eastern Slavic countries to throw coins in water at weddings—to grant protection for the newlyweds.

In the US, the two beliefs about the fountains, ponds, and lakes are common: to ensure you return and to make a special wish come true.

In all these cases, we see that people expect some kind of result from their small ritual. They might not believe in it wholeheartedly, but they still know the traditional purpose for the performed action and more or less hope that it will work. This might be a silly little tradition for most, but many of us still do it in hope of a certain outcome.

> ### *Small Spell to Find Your Special Powers*
>
> We often remember people by the peculiar, slightly quirky things they do. Things that might seem absurd if someone else did them, but, when done by that special person, they feel just right.
>
> Write a list of eleven such habits or little rituals that you'd like to be your own signature spells. You may mix the ones you already do with those you want to try out.
>
> Why eleven? It's better to give yourself some room to experiment and have options. Not every bit of magic will stick, which is completely normal.
>
> You can choose the wording for this list yourself, or, if you want, you may start by naming each habit with "My magic has many forms, and this is yet another one of them."

The Rites We Still Hold Sacred

There are also cases of true and strong belief in the power of things done in a certain way—still without the signs of a real magic ritual or witchcraft practice. Let's look at funeral rites and customs here, starting from the very essential belief that the deceased's desires concerning their funeral procedure ought to be honored and followed. This is not exclusively a religious matter: You'll find many non-religious people who feel very uneasy if their late family members' last wishes weren't followed. Of course, this may simply be a result of their respect and love of the deceased, but it is not uncommon to feel fear, anxiety, and concern about it. "He should rest properly"—you can hear lines like this even from those who, allegedly, don't believe spirits.

Additionally, lots of rituals surround death. Depending on where you are in the world, relatives open windows for the soul to fly through. They cover mirrors with cloth to prevent the spirit lingering in the house. (In some regions, this also serves as an act of protection against additional deaths in the family: The first person reflected in a mirror in the room with the coffin would be the first to die.) People wear mourning clothes and visit graveyards on certain days. And, even if the family budget is tight, many people pay quite a lot of money to ensure their relatives' graves are properly decorated, kept tidy, and visited on all the appropriate dates.

Are any of these familiar to you? Does it intuitively feel that doing things differently would be just wrong? These traditions are important to us, even though we don't know why. In fact, many want to preserve these customs so much that they have become a part of religious tradition—even though most modern religions don't actually require or mention them.

These practices and customs are somewhere on the brink of magic. They are ancient, but not forgotten, and they are still very strong and important to us. They are nourished by the limitations of our knowledge of the afterlife. What if there's really something out there? What if these traditional ways actually work and help our loved ones' souls move on? Whatever it is we believe (or whatever it is we deny)—nobody knows for sure.

The Persistence of Luck

But there is something in casual modern practices that looks even closer to real witchcraft. Something that inspires some kind of primordial confidence in magic—even if only for a moment. Let's talk about lucky charms and omens: Blowing on dice before we roll. Wearing a special item to an important event like a job interview or an exam. Looking for a traditional lucky charm, such as a four-leaf clover, a five-petal lilac flower, or a lucky number. Crossing fingers for luck. Asking friends to curse at you before an audition or test. A lot of people actually believe that these small bits of lucky magic work for them. For instance, a poll from 2018 showed that nearly a quarter of Americans wear or carry lucky charms (and who knows how many more do at least something to boost their luck, not necessarily involving a physical object).[1]

The theory of probability explains chances and odds, but it doesn't predict or rule over luck. Luck is indeed a purely irrational thing: We can win even if the chances are low. We can lose even when the odds are in our favor... It feels random, and where there's randomness, there's also magic. With luck charms and omens, we can't logically explain how they work. But we can't explain or control the randomness either! That's why a lot of people, who are in other regards rather skeptical and modern, truly believe that their lucky object will help them somehow or keep watching out for good signs, oblivious to the fact that their actions are basically a living shred of old sorcery.

So, people still do magic rituals and regard them as such! They don't necessarily call it witchcraft. But they hope it will work its magic.

---

1 Hoang Nguyen, "Nearly a Quarter of Americans Carry a Lucky Charm," YouGov, July 11, 2018, https://today.yougov.com/society/articles/21156-nearly-quarter-americans-carry-lucky-charm.

A Sliver of Ancient Irrationality

So, are we all witches and sorcerers here? This question remains a matter of philosophy and worldview. But our everyday practice shows with certainty that we definitely do some magical things which have undergone very little change throughout the ages. Be it a little tradition just for fun or some little habit in the background, it is not to be broken, just in case. A slender sliver of ancient irrationality that stays with us, that, many will say, often works.

> *Small Spell to Accept the Power of Your Lineage*
>
> Try to remember your own family traditions. Something your parents, grandparents, or other relatives may do casually, but still with a spark of irrationality and magic. The memories of this tradition might not come right away, but give yourself time and walk a bit with this question in mind. What things that seemed strangely magical and completely normal at the same time do you remember from your childhood? What customs and lore did your relatives share with you? What in your family is done in a certain way that you won't often see in other homes?
>
> Try to learn more about some of these traditions, if you can. Ask why it started, how long it's been going, and who started it.
>
> Hold everything you've learned and remembered about it close to your heart. If we're all witches in some sense, we also all have hereditary magic—and it holds a lot of power.

Between Debate and Delight

I've often seen heated discussions on social media that remind me of the fine line between witchcraft, tradition, and superstition. One side of these debates urges witchcraft practitioners to stop and repent, because they see all witchcraft practices as evil and dangerous. The other side argues that you do witchcraft, too, because even blowing out the candles on your birthday cake is witchcraft at its core. I want to say it right away, loud and clear: I am not here to rub magic in anyone's face. Because I love it too much. I love that we still have a connection with sacred practices of ancient people and can glimpse into their beliefs and experiences daily.

I simply find it beautiful. Witchcraft or not, don't you like sipping your coffee from a golden-rimmed cup, knowing your liquid black magic is safely protected from evil spirits? Wouldn't it feel nice to offer a coin to a fountain as a token of friendship to its resident water fairy? Isn't something very deep and real hidden in the most important rites in human life, from welcoming a baby to saying farewell to a deceased person? And doesn't it add meaning to streaks of luck if we know a story of how, thousands of years ago, someone else had a run of luck just like ours?

When we pay attention, we begin to see that the line between superstition, tradition, and magic is much thinner than we usually think. The habits, customs, and rituals we inherit—or adopt—carry echoes of intentions set long ago. Some are playful, some protective, some solemn, but all are threads connecting us to countless generations who acted with a mixture of hope, fear, and curiosity about the unseen.

In observing these small acts, we realize that magic is not only in the grand or dramatic gestures of witches and sorcerers, but also in the quiet ways we navigate life: stirring a drink in a certain direction, honoring a custom, or carrying a charm without fully understanding why. These are the ways the past whispers into our present, giving shape to our choices, our hopes, and our sense of wonder.

So, even if we do not call it witchcraft, we are participating in its long, subtle story. The rituals of old live on, hidden in plain sight, waiting for someone to notice, remember, or playfully honor them—and perhaps, if only for a moment, make a wish that carries a little magic of its own.

Chapter 2

What Do We Call Witchcraft?

A historical and cultural look at the many faces of witchcraft.

Witchcraft is a word loaded with mystery, fear, admiration, and misunderstanding. In this chapter, we will trace its many iterations across history and cultures, from wise women and village healers to secret societies, persecuted practitioners, and the diverse modern witches of today. We will see how the meaning of the word *witch* has shifted over time—sometimes revered, sometimes reviled, and often both at once—and how folk magic has persisted quietly through centuries of social, religious, and political change. By exploring the roots, practices, and survival of witchcraft, we can start to appreciate it and understand why it has fascinated, terrified, and inspired people for millennia.

Wise Folk Before Witch Hunts

Witchcraft has been with us for a long time. But what does this word even mean? Evil hexes? The work of wise healers? Contact with the other worlds? Let's look at the word *witch* in several different languages and try to understand its roots and meanings.

Eerie Etymology: A Witch as a Necromancer

In Old English, the word appears as *wicca* (masculine witch) and *wicce* (feminine witch). In *The American Heritage Dictionary of Indo-European Roots* (1985), Calvert Watkins traces wicca/wicce from the Proto-Indo-European root *weg-* (be strong, alive, wake) noting that wicca literally meant "one who wakes (the dead)." The *American Heritage Dictionary* also notes this *weg-* derivation and defines *wikkjaz* as a "necromancer, one who wakes the dead." This is the most widely supported tracing of the word *witch* among modern linguists.

We see necromancy as something dark, if not outright evil. But I can't help thinking about the connection between these witches who were "waking the dead" and the ancient cults of ancestors. Dead ancestors in these cults healed and blessed (as well as cursed and demanded sacrifice) and gave guidance and insight into the future. All this, with the help of people who allowed them to speak and act: ancient witches.

Germanic and Dutch Edge-Dwellers

In German and Dutch, common words for witchcraft are *Hexe* (German) and *heks* (Dutch). These words derive from the Old High German *hagzussa* or *hagazussa*, literally "hedge-sitter" or "hedge-straddler." This suggests that witches were forest women or boundary dwellers, which is reminiscent of the relatively modern concept of a folk healer and herbalist who lives at the edge of the woods and helps, among other things, with "crossing of the border" rituals, such as births or funerals.

Norse Seeresses

In Old Norse, a common word for a seeress or witch was *vǫlva* (pl. *vǫlur*), literally "staff-carrier." The word comes from Old Norse *vǫlr* "staff, distaff," implying a vǫlva is one who wields the wand of prophecy. The National Museum of Denmark notes that vǫlur were high-status women in Viking-age society. In mythic texts they were sometimes called *spákona* ("prophetess") and were always female specialists. Their graves (e.g. at Oseberg, Fyrkat, and Köpingsvik) often contain staffs and ritual objects, indicating that vǫlur were elite practitioners of magic. Ethnographically, the Norse seeress parallels the Greek *sibyl* or Slavic *ved'ma* (keep reading) as a female diviner.

Latin Witch: An Experienced Woman?

Classical Latin had the term *sāga* (also *sāgā*) meaning "wise woman" or "witch." It appears as a gloss for the Greek Λαμία, Δράκωνις, etc., and in poetry (Horace's *Epode* 5.25 mentions a witch named Saga). A derived noun *sagana* means "female diviner, soothsayer."

Latin sāga likely originally meant simply "prophetess" or "experienced woman." However, its deeper etymology is debated. In the 2014 article "*Qvae Saga, Qvis Magvs*: On the Vocabulary of the Roman Witch," Maxwell Teitel Paule points out that in different contexts sāga could mean anything from "seductress" to "experienced midwife."

Slavic Witch: The One Who Knows

In the Slavic languages, a common word for "witch" is *ved'ma* (in Czech *vědma*, in Polish *wiedźma*, in Russian ведьма, etc.), derived from the Proto-Slavic *věd-/věsti* ("to know") plus a feminine suffix. Linguists reconstruct ved'ma as *věděti-* + *-ьma*, literally "(woman) of knowledge." Thus, a ved'ma is fundamentally a "wise woman" or "seeress." The masculine form *ved'mak* (found in Polish and Ukrainian) comes from the same root ("knower").

In folklore, the Slavic witch retains this sense of someone with secret knowledge: She might heal or curse through her knowledge of herbs and fate.

* * *

So, before the witch-hunt era, "witches" typically were considered wise women, midwives, or diviners. They held ambiguous powers, being able to bless and to curse, to heal and to harm, and to tell the hidden truth or to cloud someone's judgment. They were connected with the cult of the ancestors—sometimes even "raising the dead" for the sake of the living. But as Christianity grew in power and sought to monopolize the miraculous, this view of the witch started to change for worse.

Witchcraft Persecuted

Historical Context

Witch-hunting began in late medieval Europe and grew especially intense in the 1500s through the 1600s. It gradually fading away in Europe by the end of the eighteenth century, but there are still laws against witchcraft in many countries around the world. We won't dive into historical detail here, but the anti-witch sentiment spread even further than we usually think; for example, there very few, but still some, witch trials and executions in Russia.

Legal Codification

What is important for our overview here is how the understanding of witchcraft was redefined in this process. In the fourteenth to fifteenth centuries, church doctrine reinvented witchcraft as diabolism: harmful magic (*maleficium*) practiced through a pact with Satan. This was new: Witchcraft, as people saw it, required no demonic help before.

Legal manuals like the 1487 *Malleus Maleficarum* codified this theory: It insisted witches existed, were mostly women, and learned sorcery from demons. As one infamous line put it, "three things are necessary for the effecting of witchcraft: the devil, a witch, and the Divine permission."

In other words, witches were seen as willful heretics—agents of Satan using spells, curses, or poisons to harm people and property.

Effect on Folk Practices

In practice, witchcraft accusations targeted those on society's margins: often older, unmarried, or widowed women. Those accused of witchcraft were usually *others* in their communities: They had eccentric behaviors or professions (like midwifery) that aroused suspicion.

And so, during the witch hunts, the term *witch* legally meant a person (usually a woman) believed to have consorted with the devil and used magic maliciously. But even though the word became an offense and an accusation for quite some time, the practice—and practitioners—of folk magic persisted.

Witchcraft Persisting

Italian Stregheria

In the late nineteenth century, American folklorist Charles Godfrey Leland studied and wrote about a secret community in the Italian town of Benevento. In his 1895 book *Legends of Florence*, he describes how he was initiated into the close circle of local witches who practiced *stregheria*—traditional Italian witchcraft. Its rites and knowledge were passed down through generations and were not openly taught or even discussed. The existence of the witches of Benevento was no secret. Local folklore claimed that, at night, they gathered around a big chestnut tree to perform their rituals. But what those rituals included, what practices and magic those witches possessed, nobody knew—unless they were the descendants of the older witches or, like Charles Leland, proved themselves worthy to be initiated.

This is just one of the many examples of how witchcraft practices survived, protected by secrecy and passed down in certain families.

> Old Italian witchcraft had magic battles. A lot of authors, Charles Leland and Raven Grimassi among them, have written about two rival groups of witches in traditional Italian witchcraft. The *malandanti* ("the evil walkers") hexed, cursed, and magically harmed people and their possessions. They were opposed, and kept in check, by the *benandanti* ("the good walkers"), whose main purpose was to fight the evil witches and undo their harm. Their souls would leave their bodies at night and fly to the spiritual battles with the evil forces. These battles often involved symbolic weapons like fennel stalks (benandanti) vs. sorghum stalks (malandanti).
>
> Some modern practitioners of stregheria claim to be descendants of the benandanti and carry on their traditional craft, protecting their communities and fighting evil during the night trances.

Rural Soviet Witchcraft

Another example of how amazingly resilient folk magic can be awaits us in Soviet Russia in the 1930s. The Communist Party sent groups of scientists to rural areas of the Soviet Union around this time. The purpose was twofold: research the "religious habits and other superstitions" and "educate" the people against those superstitions. The reports from these missions are proof of old folk magic having survived the Socialist revolution and persistently staying in the lives of twentieth century people. The reports were published in *Trudy po istorii i antropologii religii, 1929-1946*, a book currently in the archives of the Museum of the History of Religion in Saint Petersburg, and they show us three things—all of which are important for our understanding of how strong folk witchcraft is.

First, everyone in the rural communities knew how to practice magic. Ordinary people, working on communal farms, told the researchers how to heal the sick using local wells by addressing the spirits inhabiting them, how to lift curses with the help of a piece of cord, and many other things that we cannot call anything but village witchcraft.

Second, if things were really tricky, folks knew to talk to a full-on, skillful witch—and every village knew one. Sometimes it was a woman, but very often it was a man. Often the skilled person lived among everyone else, but some villages didn't have their own miracle workers and had to rely on the touring ones. Happily for them, traveling witches weren't rare and were basically local celebrities. They performed more specialized magic: powerful healing, herbalism, and sometimes even performed their magic with the help of bees (this was rather popular as bees and bee products were seen as carrying otherworldly powers).

Third, local Orthodox Christian priests also performed some kinds of folk magic for people in need. When the church was a strong authority, it was uncommon for priests to perform rituals that were not part of a religious canon. But when both religion and folk magic were suppressed by the Soviet Union authorities, reports of priests providing healing and traditional ceremonies with clear pagan roots became more numerous. With the church defunded, priests became fully dependent on the people's help and support, and that influenced their range of services: they were more willing to do anything that people wanted and loved. And people really loved magic.

This kind of folk witchcraft, miraculously preserved since pagan times, has survived both Christianity and communism. It is still common to know a practitioner of such magic, especially in rural areas. They aren't usually called *witches* these days. Sometimes these people are known as *koldovka* (a female witch) or *koldun* (a male witch). But most often they are referred to simply as "that one who can do stuff," "the skillful one," or just *babka* ("elderly woman").

So, even when the very word *witch* becomes almost forbidden, the witches' craft lives on, through any political, social, and religious context.

Witchcraft Reconstructed

The Secret Religion of Witches?

The old ways of the witches are captivating, and, with the rise of anthropology in the twentieth century, the interest in witchcraft has grown as well. Many scholars wanted to research and reconstruct the system of practices that were almost eradicated by alliances between churches and governments. In fact, the fascination with that old, "authentic" witchcraft was so great that it created a demand to go further than just regular academic research of practices, backed by historical and archaeological evidence. People wanted to know the ideology behind these practices. They wanted to discover the religion of the witches.

There weren't, and still aren't, nearly enough facts to do such a thing. But some enthusiastic researchers still tried, and, thanks to them, we now have a whole religion: undeniably modern but inspired by real witches' practices...and the twentieth century's human's imagination, full of longing for the forgotten old ways. Of course, I am talking about Wicca.

The Birth and Rise of Wicca

Wicca was presented to the public by Gerald Gardner in the 1950s, but under the names Craft of the Wise, Witchcraft, and the Witch-cult. In the 1960s, it became known as Wicca. Nowadays, Wiccan and witch aren't necessarily the same thing: You can be a witch but not define yourself as a follower of Wicca.

I am not a Wiccan, though I deeply respect this spiritual tradition. So it is not my place to describe the details and teachings of the religion I know only from books. What I want to emphasize is that Wicca has brought us renewed awareness of nature's magic and of the fluid, multifaceted essence of divinity—and all that still shapes a lot of modern witches' practices, even if they aren't Wiccan themselves.

Many Faces of Modern Witchcraft

Countless Varieties of Modern Practice

Some modern witches call themselves witches. Some don't. We can still see witchcraft as a social role: a wise person, helping others through a combination of magic, empathy, and natural remedies. Happily, a lot of witches in this sense are still here, helping where they are needed. They might or might not call themselves witches, but they definitely play this role and continue the unbroken tradition (or maybe many different traditions).

There are also a lot of people (myself among them) who call themselves witches. We all are very different, and free to choose any way of being a witch we like best.

I'll tell you about several branches of modern witchcraft, but it is very important to understand several things about them. First, this is an unofficial categorization: It is based on what we feel or practice and does not require membership or certifications. Second, different "types" of witches are hardly divided at all! We often have more than one "witchcraft identity," because they aren't at all mutually exclusive. Finally, this is by no means a comprehensive list. I doubt there *can* be a complete list, as modern witchcraft is so diverse, nuanced, and multifaceted. So, what kinds of witchcraft, among many others, exist and thrive in the modern world?

* * *

Hereditary Witchcraft: Magical practices passed down through family lineage or bloodline.

Folk Witchcraft: Traditional, often rural magic rooted in local customs and remedies.

Green Witchcraft: Nature-based magic focused on herbs, plants, and earth energy.

Neo-Pagan Witchcraft: Modern spiritual practices drawing from ancient pagan beliefs, often including Wicca.

Divination Witchcraft: Magic centered on gaining insight through tools like tarot, runes, or scrying.

Lunar Witchcraft: Witchcraft that works with moon phases and lunar energy.

Solar Witchcraft: Magic that harnesses the power and symbolism of the sun.

Kitchen Witchcraft: Everyday magic practiced through cooking, food, and household rituals.

Cosmic Witchcraft: Practices involving celestial bodies, astrology, and cosmic energy.

Mind Witchcraft: Magic focused on mental influence, visualization, and psychic abilities. Often includes meditation, affirmations, and manifesting.

Crystal Witchcraft: Witchcraft which uses crystals and gemstones for healing, protection, and energy work.

Chaotic Witchcraft: Magic that is flexible, rule-breaking, and blends various magical systems freely and recognizes no absolute authority.

Witchcraft of the Dead: Practices involving communication with the souls of the deceased, mediumship, and honoring the dead.

Ancestral Witchcraft: Magic focused on connecting with, understanding, and drawing power from our bloodlines.

Ritual Witchcraft: Magic focused on structured, ceremonial practices often involving set tools, steps, and timing.

Love Witchcraft: Practices that use spells and energies to attract, enhance, influence, or understand love and relationships.

Witchcraft of the Word: Witchcraft centered on the magical power of spoken or written language, such as chants, charms, or carefully crafted verbal spells and incarnations.

Eclectic Witchcraft: Personalized practices that draw from multiple traditions and systems without sticking strictly to one path.

> *Small Spell to Become a Witch from the Past, Reborn*
>
> Recall or find a piece of your local folklore about witches or any other people of magical power. Examine it a bit more closely than you have before. Don't take it for granted, but really look at this belief, story, or even recipe or ritual, preserved in time. Try to see what it could mean, what else it could tell you, apart from the obvious.
>
> If you want to, try to embody, recreate or "try on" something from this piece of lore. Now you are the witch—connected briefly and minutely to the old ways.

Folk Magic: The Craft We Were Born With

I particularly want to highlight and emphasize various folk practices. They are unique not only to each country, but also to different regions; each area can have its own magic, its own rituals, and its own memories of special practitioners who were more capable than the rest. These practices are all around us: They are a living part of the experience of almost every person. They have always been here, and we can always rely on their wisdom or be inspired by their mysterious and still familiar charm.

Some of these traditions and practices are even prohibited and persecuted (unfortunately, this is still happening), yet they continue to live on in defiance of this spiritual oppression. Other magical practices, on the contrary, are being revived and becoming quite trendy.

Wherever we go, there is lively, real, and unique witchcraft that we can practice consciously—or absorb unnoticed—through traditions and customs.

* * *

The story of witchcraft is not only about fear, persecution, and superstition. It is a story of resilience and continuity. From the wise women and seers of the past to the eclectic, modern witches of today, the craft has survived countless changes in society, religion, and politics. It lives on quietly in local traditions, in whispered knowledge, in the small, everyday magic of our surroundings. By understanding its history, we see that witchcraft is not a relic, but a living expression of human ingenuity, curiosity, and desire to connect with the unseen. Whether consciously practiced or subtly absorbed, it remains a thread linking past and present, reminding us that the extraordinary can coexist with the ordinary…and that the powers of knowledge, intuition, and ritual have never truly left the world.

Small Spell to Officially Become a Wise Witch

A witch can mean someone of knowledge. Light a candle, take a moment of peace and silence, and write down all the things you have knowledge about. What are you an expert on? What are you skilled at? What unusual things do you know or can do? This list should be long, so don't stop at the obvious. Dig deeper and remember even the smallest special skills and interests.

You are not so simple, are you?

Chapter 3

The Human Mind in Search of Meaning and Mystery

A sweeping overview of magical practices from prehistory to today—why we've always sought the sacred.

The mysterious, the unseen, the sacred… Why is all of this so appealing to us? This chapter explores that long, winding journey, from the first cave paintings to modern digital rituals, tracing how magic, in its many forms, has shaped the ways we understand the world and ourselves. We will see that magic is not merely superstition or error; it is a deeply human impulse, a way to create meaning, cope with uncertainty, and connect to something larger than our everyday lives. By looking at prehistoric mindscapes, ancient civilizations, secret esoteric paths, and the modern resurgence of magical practices, we can begin to understand why, even today, the human mind continues to seek the numinous. This chapter is an invitation to see magic not as a curiosity of the past, but as an active plot line in the ongoing story of humanity's search for wonder, purpose, and transcendence.

Magic as a Mistake

It is quite obvious that people, as a species, have always needed the sacred, and this need is deeper and more existential than many would think. The typical, modern pop culture explanation of how magic initially appeared in human life is usually quite condescending: Ancient people were afraid of nature's forces and had close to no control over them, so they had to explain everything as the work of spirits or gods. They tried irrational, false-logic ways to influence these imaginary forces. The lightning frightened them, and (having no idea where it came from) they decided it was a sign from the spirits or the work of a thunder god. They depended on rain so fully that the idea of having no control over it was too much to bear, so they invented rituals, imitating rain falling on the earth. The human mind has always sought reason and control, and, where control was limited, humanity invented at least a parody of it. This explanation might have something truth to it, but it is obviously not complete. Because if it were, then why would we still pray to gods, do any rituals, stick to any spiritual or religious paths, or even immerse ourselves in fantasy worlds, somehow almost believing in their reality? Now that we have modern science and a bit of control over the nature's forces, we ought to stop with all the magic, right? But the thing is—we don't.

The Need for the Numinous

From the very beginning, humans have sought the sacred—and haven't ever really stopped. The numinous is a whole category of human experience which connects us to the divine reality.

Mircea Eliade, who researched that very need for the sacred, the magical, and the supernatural notes that there's more than one reason for that.

For instance, we all need the sacred as an opposition to the profane. We tend to get tired of the visible, easily perceived, and repetitive reality we all experience day to day. There are many things we don't understand, approve of, or agree with in it. That's why we seek to balance it with another kind of reality: the sacred one. If we lack order, fairness, meaning, or beauty, we construct them as ideas and hopes and put them into that metaphysical, spiritual, sacred space. We've been doing this for quite some time as a species. The density and vastness of this collectively created and shared metaphysical reality has become a matter of study on its own—for example, as the Collective Consciousness in Carl Jung's works. All in all, when we see the unusual, we often fear it and are intrigued by it at the same time. Such is the double nature of anything magical.

Then, we need to—let's say it in a modern way—romanticize our whole existence as humans on this earth. And this demand created origin myths—one of the pillars of our spiritual history. Myths of origin were created, retold, and reenacted. Whole religions were based on them, and numerous ritual practices emerged from them... The sacred stories of how this world was created, and how and why we humans got invited to live here, gave meaning and solid ground for the mind, literally and figuratively keeping incalculable generations of people sane and content.

And last but not least, we have always sought transcendence. Or, simply put, some kind of immortality and continuity. We know that life is finite, and that is a hard truth. Coping with it can look different: from believing in a full-scale afterlife to seeing life as a constant cycle of reincarnation or worshipping nature and being ready to participate in its circle of life and death. All of these attitudes, and many others, call for different spiritual worldviews, different concepts about the sacred and eternal. Connecting with something timeless is so dear to the human mind exactly because it is not timeless at all. Eternity is a concept we all can get hypnotized by—in ancient and modern times alike.

> *Small Spell for Immortality*
>
> Pick an object that you think will transcend your own life, that is likely to outlive you and everyone you know. This might be a rock, a book, a piece of jewelry, a figurine, a photograph, a diary...
>
> Start telling things to this object—something that you'd like to pass on to eternity, or at least to a very distant future. Ask this object to remember what you tell it and to keep your living thoughts forever.

Prehistoric Mindscapes

Before any cities or temples existed, humans were already reaching for something bigger than themselves. We see this in the oldest places they left their mark—deep inside caves and beneath the earth in early graves.

In caves like Lascaux in France or Altamira in Spain, prehistoric people painted animals—bison, horses, deer—with incredible detail and care. Were they doodles for amusement and passing the time? Or some kind of hunting wikiHow? Many researchers believe these paintings were part of rituals, maybe even early attempts to connect with a spirit world. Art was basically magic in the beginning.

Burial sites from tens of thousands of years ago tell a similar story. Bodies were placed carefully, sometimes with red ochre, tools, or ornaments. These acts suggest that early humans believed in an afterlife...or at least that death meant more than just the end. Even then, people were searching for meaning beyond what they could see.

At the heart of all this is a way of thinking called animism—the belief that everything in nature has a spirit. Trees, rivers, animals, and even rocks could be alive in some mysterious way—and, of course, the souls of humans themselves after they pass away. This made the world feel enchanted and full of hidden meaning.

These ancient practices show us something timeless: early people were already asking big questions about life, death, and what might lie beyond.

Magic as Meaning-Making

So what is magic, exactly? Unlike religion, which often involves gods and moral rules, or science, which relies on testing and evidence, magic is more direct and personal. It's the idea that certain actions or symbols can influence the world in hidden ways. Say a charm to protect your home or bless your meal—that's magic in action.

Modern scholars often focus on rituals as forms of communication. Communication with what exactly? Well, with the spirits or supernatural forces, of course—but not exclusively. For example, Victor Turner, along with other authors, sees magic as a way to mark a transformation (for example, coming of age, healing, or the beginning of a new cycle). The power of such magic is as much in the performance and shared belief as in the otherworldly forces. This way of looking at ancient magical rituals suggests that magic is a means to communicate important ideas to the self and to the community. That's probably why even the people who don't believe in anything supernatural still participate in rituals with clear (or, sometimes, not so clear) magical roots.

The Sacred in Early Civilizations

As cities rose and writing appeared, humans didn't leave magic and mystery behind. Instead, they built entire civilizations around them. In ancient Mesopotamia, Egypt, the Indus Valley, and Mesoamerica, the sacred was woven into daily life, politics, art, and architecture.

Priests held real power—not just spiritual, but political. In many cultures, they were seen as a bridge between humans and the gods. Temples were, of course, places to worship, but they were also centers of knowledge, law, entertainment, and even science. Divination—reading signs from the stars, animals, or the movement of oil in water—was a respected way to make decisions.

In Mesopotamia and Mesoamerica, astrology flourished. People watched the skies not just for timekeeping, but to understand fate. The Egyptians saw the stars and afterlife as deeply connected, and their temples were often aligned with celestial events. In the Indus Valley, while we know less due to their language being untranslatable, symbols and city planning suggest a strong spiritual framework.

Even alchemy—mixing metals and seeking immortality—began as a sacred practice, tied to the idea that the physical and spiritual worlds were one.

For these ancient cultures, the sacred was much more real than for most modern people: It shaped cities, kingship, and the stars above. It made the world feel knowable and full of purpose.

> Some things from the ancient times stay with us even today, but others change completely.
>
> These days, in magical circles, it is often believed that the scariest rituals are those which involve the dead—cemetery magic and such. Meanwhile, invoking gods is safe and beneficial and seen as something you can do for any occasion. But in fact, this is most likely the result of how our consciousnesses has been shaped by Christianity (where Jesus is definitely safe and available for any prayer, open to all).
>
> In antiquity, however, gods were actually invoked less often than spirits of the dead: It was reasonably assumed that gods

> were more powerful—meaning more dangerous—and that it was best not to annoy them with requests. The dead, on the other hand, were harmless enough and often bored in the afterlife, so they didn't mind carrying out a magical task for a small offering or even just for fun. In its own way, this makes a lot of sense, even though it doesn't go along with our modern thinking.

Mystery Cults and Esoteric Traditions

Not all sacred paths were public: some traditions offered secret knowledge to a chosen few. These were the mystery cults and esoteric teachings of the ancient world.

In Greece, the Eleusinian Mysteries promised a deeper understanding of life, death, and rebirth. Participants went through secret rituals that were never written down.

Later, movements like Gnosticism and Kabbalah focused on hidden truths. Gnostics believed that divine knowledge could free the soul from a broken world. Kabbalists searched for spiritual meaning in the Hebrew language and the structure of the universe, aspiring to eventually heal the universe.

These paths shared key ideas: inner change, initiation into secret wisdom, and the belief that symbols could reveal higher truths and even serve the higher purpose of mending the flaws of our world.

Silence and mystery were part of the journey. What mattered was not just believing, but also experiencing something sacred from within.

Through these traditions, people looked inward to find the divine—and to unlock hidden layers of reality.

Rationalism Meets the Occult

During the Enlightenment, thinkers in Europe began to favor reason, science, and logic. Superstition was seen as backward. Magic, alchemy, and astrology were pushed aside. The world was being reimagined as a machine, not a mystery or a divine story.

But the magic didn't end there. In the eighteenth and nineteenth centuries, the Romantic movement brought a wave of new interest in myth, mystery, and the spiritual world. Artists, poets, and thinkers felt that cold reason wasn't enough. They longed for wonder, intuition, and a sense of the sacred. Folklore was being collected, researched, and admired.

Art and poetry from the nineteenth century's romantics sometimes sound and look like true spells, like pieces of real magic today.

Here are some examples from William Butler Yeats:

"The world is full of magic things, patiently waiting for our senses to grow sharper."

✱ ✱ ✱

> "Faeries, come take me out of this dull world,
>
> For I would ride with you upon the wind,
>
> Run on the top of the dishevelled tide,
>
> And dance upon the mountains like a flame."
>
> * * *
>
> "Let us go forth, the tellers of tales, and seize whatever prey the heart long for, and have no fear. Everything exists, everything is true, and the earth is only a little dust under our feet."
>
> **These lines bring true living magic closer to us, no matter when we read them.**

Soon, occult ideas returned in new forms. Groups like the Theosophical Society and the Hermetic Order of the Golden Dawn explored ancient wisdom, ritual magic, and spiritual symbols. These groups blended Eastern philosophies, Western mysticism, and psychology.

In the twentieth century, Carl Jung gave new life to these ideas with his concept of archetypes—symbols shared across cultures and dreams. For Jung, exploring the subconscious was a way to connect with the mystical parts of the self.

Even in an age of science, magic remains. People continue to look for meaning not solely in facts, but in symbols, visions, and hidden truths as well.

Magic of the Modern Mind

Today, magic has taken on some new forms...along with persisting in its ancient ways somewhere in the background. In fact, many people are turning to magic and spirituality to make sense of a fast-moving, uncertain world.

Neo-pagan movements like Wicca have brought forth old gods, seasonal rituals, and nature-based magic. Practitioners honor the cycles of the moon, cast spells, and celebrate ancient festivals with a modern twist. Chaos magic and eclectic witchcraft take an even more flexible approach, treating belief itself as a tool: If it works, it's real enough.

> Many things that look modern have historical precedent and aren't new age inventions.
>
> For instance, an eclectic mishmash of gods and goddesses from different pantheons isn't something that Wiccans created. This was done even in antiquity: sometimes, people back then would literally invoke every suitable deity they knew of.
>
> Here's a fragment of an incantation from a Hellenistic ritual, which I translated from the original Russian, in the 2019 book *Ancient Magic: A Practitioner's Guide to the Supernatural in Greece and Rome* by Philip Matyszak:

> "Sown by Cronus, conceived by Hera, nurtured by Amun and born of Isis, you were nourished by Zeus, bringer of moisture, and raised by the sun and dew..."
>
> Here you can see that Greek and Egyptian gods peacefully live side by side in this piece of old magic.

Magic has also slipped into everyday life through self-help and manifestation. Ideas like "what you think, you attract" borrow from older magical thinking but now come wrapped in glossy books and viral TikToks.

The internet has become a new kind of sacred space. People create digital altars, share spells online, and even follow algorithm-driven astrology. Social media shapes belief, spreads symbols, and connects seekers across the globe.

In the modern mind, magic is often personal and therapeutic, but it's also easy and recreational. It blends ancient ideas with memes and screenshots. Whether serious or symbolic, it still helps people feel connected, empowered, and part of something bigger than themselves.

When life feels unstable—during wars, pandemics, or personal struggles—people often turn to magic, spirituality, or ritual for comfort and clarity. These practices offer a sense of control, connection, and meaning when the world feels too big or fast-paced to grasp.

Magic, in all its forms, is a tool for resilience. Whether by casting a spell, lighting a candle, or repeating a mantra, people create a sense of order and purpose. It's not always about supernatural belief. Sometimes, it's just about finding a moment of focus in the chaos.

As science and technology shape more of our lives, the sacred doesn't vanish—it changes form. Tarot apps, AI-generated horoscopes, and online rituals are new versions of very old needs. They show that humans are not purely logical beings; we are also symbolic ones. We crave story, we make up meaning, we love a good mystery…

This "sacred instinct" may be hardwired into us. Our brains are built to find patterns, tell stories, and imagine what lies beyond. From cave paintings to quantum mysticism, we've always used imagination to stretch beyond the visible world. Magic, then, is not a superstition. It's a deeply human response to the unknown—and a subconscious prayer to the beautiful irrationality of this world.

Through time, from the caves of prehistory to the bustling digital spaces of today, magic has endured not because it is clever trickery or a deep delusion, but because it fulfills a deeply human need: to find meaning, to reach beyond the visible, and to touch something timeless. It has taken countless forms: rituals, spells, myths, secret teachings, and modern practices. Still, its essence remains the same: a bridge between the known and the unknown, the ordinary and the sacred. By tracing these threads, we see that magic is a living expression of our desire to understand, to live on with meaning and purpose, and to connect. And even as the world changes, that impulse has never left us. Instead, it adapts, waiting quietly in the corners of everyday life, ready to emerge whenever we need it most.

Chapter 4

Seasonal Rituals

*Halloween, winter holidays, and other favorite festivities—
how ancient celebrations live on in our calendars and homes.*

Most of us know, of course, that some of our modern-day holidays and celebrations stem from older festivals. It is commonly recognized now that Halloween is a descendant of the pagan-Celtic *Samhain* and that, before Christmas (or other winter holidays) was celebrated, the winter solstice (or Yule) held its place.

But some other connections between now and back then aren't so well-known. For example, St Valentine's Day is rarely considered in the broader context of February's holidays in different pagan cultures—from ancient Roman *Lupercalia* to Celtic *Imbolc*. And in fact, these traditions are all connected, all celebrating purification and love.

Another example is the May 1 Labor Day, which is a big deal (and, ironically, a state holiday) all throughout Russia and the Balkans. It is usually celebrated in nature, around the fire (or a grill), and still carries, subtly and stealthy, a lot of meaning and traditions from its older versions—be it a pagan one from ancient Roman, Celtic, or even Medieval Christian.

Even though we know that our holidays connect us to history, we rarely think about their magic. Festivals and celebrations were magical events with certain rituals, each of which had its own purpose, and this was clear and vital for everyone.

We still perform these rituals. We mostly do them for entertainment, to feel the atmosphere of the season, to bring back childhood memories, or just because everyone does it. But these are the very actions that once were believed to be sacred, important, and highly effective.

Do they still carry this magic? It mostly depends on the intention we put into them. A Christmas wreath on our door might be just a decoration, a small, cute tradition, a token of how much we love Christmas…or (why not?) it may still be the powerful sacred symbol of rebirth and eternity, ensuring the solar year's restart and promising immortality to our souls.

Let's take a closer look at our calendar and its celebrations. Be sure: We'll find a lot of magical meaning and ancient enchantment there.

Samhain, Halloween, and More

We're starting with Halloween not because it's the most obviously witchy holiday out there, but because historical predecessors of this celebration marked it as the beginning of the year.

I'm talking mostly about Celtic Samhain, of course—but not exclusively.

On a bronze plaque with a list of months made in the second century CE by the Gauls (known as the Coligny calendar), one of the months is *Samonios*. This is evidence that most likely Samhain (literally meaning "summer's end") existed not only among Celts, but among the Gauls as well.

In the Eastern and Western Slavic countries, there was a holiday with a different name but the same idea: When the border thins between seasons, years, and worlds, we need to honor our dead loved ones and ancestors. This holiday was called *Dedy* (*Dziady*), meaning literally, "The Grandfathers," but referring to all ancestors. Among the Southern Slavic peoples, the same tradition was called *Zadushnitsa* ("for the souls").

Both Dedy and Zadushnitsa took place several times a year—always in the liminal times between seasons or other important elements of the yearly cycle. But one of these times was always in the late autumn: at the end of October or the beginning of November. The main tradition was to honor the ancestors and their burial sites—just as with Samhain.

It seems that all these, and many other, holidays remembering the dead in the late autumn all stem from the common ancient Indo-European ritual cycle.

In the eighth century CE, Pope Gregory III moved the All Saints' (or All Hallows') Day from May 13 to November 1, along with All Souls Day moving to November 2. Maybe it was done to replace the pagan Samhain celebration with the Christian one, but with both holidays being centered around the supernatural forces and honoring the dead ancestors, the two traditions fused together. And that, through time and tradition, brought us the modern-day All Hallow's Eve or Halloween, the most obviously magical, witchy, and spooky holiday.

The Magic and Meaning of Samhain

Samhain was seen as a liminal time, a triple border between summer and winter, the last year and the new one, and our human world and the world of the souls of the dead, fairy folk, and gods.

On this border, things get fluid and unstable, increasing the possibility of meeting the spirits of your deceased relatives, as well as any other visitors from the spiritual realm, malicious or benevolent.

Connecting with the dead and with the underworld presented opportunities: Divination was more accurate than the rest of the year, and communication with deceased relatives became easy (so they could pass on some requests, and the living could ask for ancestral blessing and protection).

The night before November 1 was also seen as a deadline: You had to finish harvesting your crops by then, and anything that was left unharvested belonged to the fairy folk.

Why All the Pumpkins?

Actually, there were no pumpkins—there was not a single pumpkin in Europe until sixteenth century!

To ward off unwelcome spirits on Samhain, Celts carved grotesque faces into turnips or other root vegetables and placed embers or candles inside to create lanterns. Later, these were called "jack-o'-lanterns," when they were linked to an Irish folktale about a soul named Stingy Jack who tricked the devil and was doomed to wander the earth with only a carved-out turnip lantern. But this legend was an explanation of the much older traditional use of vegetable lanterns, created when the need for protection against spirits was forgotten.

When Irish immigrants came to America, they adapted the tradition using pumpkins, which were larger and easier to carve.

So, the original magical meaning of carving Halloween pumpkins is protection. Placed by the windows, they signal that there is enough scary stuff inside already; any spirits should walk by and leave this household alone. Warding off unwanted spirits or energy is an all-time necessity, so we can carve our pumpkins with this intention in mind and make our Halloween celebration more purposeful and satisfying.

Trick-or-Treating

During Samhain, sweet treats were offered to the spirits and souls of the dead to honor or appease them. And to ward off evil spirits, some people dressed as evil spirits themselves.

This looks almost like modern trick-or-treating, but without the key element: people asking for treats for themselves. But, as we'll see later, this custom is ancient as well. A version became quite popular in medieval Europe with the Souling custom from the ninth to fifteenth centuries. Poor people offered to pray for the souls of the deceased in exchange for cakes.

This tradition evolved, and, by the 1930s, children in the US began dressing up and asking for sweets. The phrase "trick or treat" became popular by the 1950s.

* * *

But things are not that simple—let's look into the very essence of this custom. For that, we need to travel to Sicily, to the celebration of All Souls' Day on November 2—the traditions of this holiday have been preserved and performed right up to the present day.

At dawn, children receive a basket of sweets. With this basket, they go around to their relatives, saying: "Look what beautiful *dead ones* were brought to me!" The adults reply: "The dead sent you the *dead ones*!" The "dead ones" in the basket are sweets shaped like bones or little human figures. They are usually in very bright, cheerful colors: red, yellow, orange, and purple. After the children have shown off their gifts, they should eat them, while adults are not allowed to. The reason is that in certain cultures children are associated with the dead—they are closer to that boundary between being and non-being than adults. It was also believed that the dead return to the world of the living by being born again. In agrarian symbolism, children play the same role as seeds of plants—they help life to be renewed. And so they can represent the dead in the world of the living—as the closest to them in status and association. By letting children eat the ritual sweets, adults in fact offer the sweets to the dead (the departed "eat" through the children's mouths).

And by receiving sweets as gifts "from the dead," children symbolically accept the blessings that the living expect from their ancestors: strength and protection.

* * *

By the way, in that same category of those "close to the dead" were sometimes included old people, beggars, the sick, and the disabled (here we can recall again the medieval custom of Souling). We can still see this connection with our own eyes, because in some places offerings of food or money to such people remain part of funerary or commemorative rituals. In this way, offerings to the dead are passed through them.

Many anthropologists, for example O. D. Fais-Leutskaya, point out that if children participate ritually in a commemorative ceremony, this is a direct sign of the archaic nature of that rite. In Sicily on All Souls' Day (also called the Sugar Night), this has been preserved in its direct form, while in the trick-or-treating of Halloween we find its echo. Adults are obliged to put sweets in children's baskets or else risk misfortune—that is the exact shape of the ancient rituals for the dead. Their original purpose was to appease the dead, with children acting as intermediaries. Today, hardly anyone thinks of Halloween traditions this way, at least not literally. But the actions themselves are preserved, carried unchanged (though with long interruptions in certain regions) through centuries and millennia. So, if someone says that Halloween only exists so that food corporations can sell more candy—remember that going door to door demanding treats is way, way more ancient than capitalism.

Parties and Merriment

Loud Halloween parties and wild fun are somewhat traditional and ancient too. Back in the pagan days, people used songs, laughter, and jokes to repel the evil.

Later, the church issued prohibitions against the street celebrations and merriment on the All Hallows' Eve, so we know the fun had continued. So, Halloween becoming one of the biggest modern holidays is logical: First, people *had* to have fun, and then, they just really liked it.

Divination

Tarot readings and Ouija board sessions on Halloween are somewhat common now. Many people do this for fun—especially those who don't practice such things in their daily lives. Halloween parties often have an invited tarot practitioner, and it is generally agreed that, even if you don't feel good about fortune-telling, on Halloween it is somehow okay.

But is that the real spirit of ancient Samhain? In fact, it is—but the methods of divination were very different, as well as the questions being asked.

Most authentic Samhain divination techniques were meant to answer only one question, a most simple and grim one: "Will I die this year?" It mattered a lot for people back then, right before another cold, cruel winter, when, sadly, many perished from hunger. There were numerous ways for the spirits to show an answer to this question. For example, after the big Samhain bonfire burned down, everyone left their footprints in the ashes. If, by morning, your footprint was still there, untouched, you would live through the year successfully. But if the footprint was smudged or wiped off, it was time to prepare yourself…

So, the questions that we ask the spiritual world on Halloween have changed, but the tradition itself is still in place. It seems that we still believe, even if only subconsciously, that the other realm actually becomes closer to our world on that night. So, we are just like the Celts leaving footprints in ashes with very important questions in mind.

Visiting the Cemetery

The exact dates may vary, but in many different countries, cultures, and religions, people visit their relatives' graves in late October and early November. Modern-day Halloween celebrations don't include visiting the cemetery (if they do, it's usually for the spooky atmosphere). But there are special days like All Souls' Day (on November 2) in Catholicism or Parents' Saturday (first Saturday of November) in Orthodox Christianity.

It is very important to see this connection and let it sink in: Many of us still act upon the ancient belief that the souls of the dead get closer to us around the day we now call Halloween and that they, somehow, become available for contact and are probably waiting for acts of love and respect from their descendants.

Symbols of Halloween

Everything we now see as a symbol of Halloween is, very likely, connected to Samhain and its strong magic.

Bats, black cats and dogs, spiders, frogs and toads, owls, ravens—these aren't simply "scary animals." There was a belief that, on the night of Samhain, powerful sorcerers and witches could shapeshift into certain animals. Yes, exactly those animals that are now associated with Halloween!

Cauldrons and potions are memories of actual witches, who could heal or poison people using their medicinal craft.

Pumpkins, even though not known to Celts, are still a symbol of harvest: the very harvest that everyone had to collect from the fields before Samhain.

And all kinds of ghosts, ghouls, skeletons, zombies, vampires, mummies, and so forth are very clear memories of the core meaning of Samhain: the veil get thin and the spirits walk among us.

Small Spell to Do on October 31

This is how you invite ghosts to dinner: cook in silence, set the table for more people than you are expecting, open the windows to invite the spirits in, and don't talk while you eat. After your dinner, close the windows with blessings and gratitude (not just because it's polite; this would be the ghosts' cue to leave).

The Winter Solstice: Yule and Other Winter Holidays

It was celebrated all around the northern hemisphere: the longest night and the shortest day of the year. The winter solstice. It is likely the most ancient celebration of the whole hemisphere. Many different traditions of honoring this celestial event are known to history. For example, Saturnalia, a whole week of ancient Roman festivities, started before the solstice and ended right after. It was held to honor the god Saturn and included traditions that would seem very familiar to a modern-day reader: public festivals, private feasts, and gift giving.

Celtic Yule, in some ways, was similar to the Saturnalia: It lasted for a week, included feasts and gifts... Every culture had its own winter solstice celebration customs, but I will focus on Yule. We'll see the most parallels between it and our own familiar modern winter holidays.

Let's look at the elements of Yule and see what stayed and what was (almost) forgotten.

The Battle Between the Light and the Darkness

...Which the light wins. There was a folk belief about the fight between the Oak King and the Holly King, which happened every solstice. The Holly King represented darkness, night, winter, and death. He won every summer solstice, so the sun began to die, and the days dwindled. The Oak King stood for light, day, summer, and life. His victory took place every winter solstice, promising the rebirth of the sun and the lengthening of the day. This legend isn't a part of modern winter holiday lore, but there is one important element here: the birth of the new sun. This motif is so universal and powerful because we see it with our own eyes: The days do become longer after the winter solstice. And this fact has numerous mythological and religious interpretations throughout the history.

Who was that sacred newborn sun who came to this world at the end of December to fight evil and darkness? You might have thought Jesus Christ, and you would be totally right! But...what if I told you that he isn't the only one, according to other religions? For instance, the birthday of Mithra, the ancient Iranian solar god, also happened just around the winter solstice. By the way, he was a god of many good things at once: light, friendship, oaths, contracts, and justice. He was even depicted with the twelve zodiac signs, which somewhat corresponds with the twelve apostles.

What's really worth mentioning here is the fact that the newborn solar god was celebrated around the winter solstice, and this tradition went on and on. Many will say that it has been fully preserved well into modern times.

Regardless of what religion or worldview you prefer, the light gets reborn at the end of December and, we hope, everything good and kind with it.

We even honor this quite literally! Most wintertime traditional decor is connected with light: candles, Christmas lights, glowing lawn decorations...and, of course, the warm and cozy light of the fireplace.

Wreaths and Garlands: Are They Ancient, Too?

Floral wreaths existed in many cultures. They are not specific to winter holidays—for example, they are a big part of Eastern Slavic Midsummer celebrations and modern Southern Slavic Easter. It is not a coincidence that the wreath appears in connection with solar festivals: solstices and equinoxes. Because the round wreath is, of course, a little model of the sun. It is meant to represent the sun's journey: its birth, its travel through the sky, its disappearance and resurrection.

So, your Christmas wreath still bears that ancient symbolism: the circle of life, cycles of renewal, and, most importantly, immortality.

Garlands carry a much darker history and meaning. They originate from the guts of the sacrificial animals which were hung on the fir trees after their sacrifice as a sign of our human commitment to the divine and our readiness to share our wealth. What a journey from poor animals' intestines to jolly decorations! But it's important to see the sacred meaning this held for ancient people: sacrifice, faith, sharing, commitment...and accepting the death of one thing to nurture another.

Feast and Gifts: More than Just Fun and Good Memories

For the ancient Celts (and not them alone), the winter solstice was a scary time. It was cold, dark, and food supplies often started to grow scarce around this time. People were afraid and well aware of the danger that they simply would not survive the winter. The Yule celebration was there to help the community, or to be more accurate, to let the community help itself, especially those who were in the direst need.

On Yule, those households that had some spare food (more than just to live through the winter) brought it out and left under the trees—so those who didn't have enough to sustain themselves could still have a chance. So, the gifts were not for fun and pleasant memories. They were someone's only chance to survive.

The Yule feast was just another form of sharing and redistributing the wealth gained through summer and autumn. Those who could contribute a significant amount of food to the feast were regarded with great respect, and it was an honorable thing to do. So, the spirit of sharing is not exclusive to modern Christmas and has been there long before Charles Dickens enlightened Ebenezer Scrooge on this matter.

Who Is Santa?

In Russia where I grew up, we had Ded Moroz (Grandfather Frost) instead of Santa Claus. He is a Soviet invention but with some roots in actual Eastern Slavic folklore. Two winter spirits were known there: Moroz and Karachun. Basically, they represented "the cold" and "the freaking deadly freezing cold." Moroz was relatively benevolent and could bring gifts to those who had been polite to him. Karachun was terrible (but still admired).

The carnivalesque winter festivities and traditions were meant to cajole him and keep him away at the same time. When in the twentieth century Ded Moroz was created as a new, religion-free version of Santa, he became a mixture of ancient Moroz and (in lesser proportion) Karachun.

In ancient Rome, the winter solstice was dedicated to Saturn—a god who represented antiquity, time, labor, and the long-gone golden age of early agricultural living before civilizations and cities emerged. Saturn was depicted as an old man.

In Norse mythology, the god Odin was connected with the winter solstice. During the darkest nights of the year, he was believed to lead the Wild Hunt, a ghostly procession through the sky. According to folklore, Odin flew through the night sky on his eight-legged horse Sleipnir, visiting homes and observing people's behavior—a role that oddly mirrored the modern Santa Claus myth. People would leave offerings—sometimes food or straw for Sleipnir—which echoes the practice of leaving treats for Santa and his reindeer. And yes, Odin was also depicted as an old (though still strong and powerful) man.

So, what's with all the "grandpa" figures around the winter solstice? Why do we see it in different cultures, myths, and contexts, all around the northern hemisphere? And where do all these fascinating parallels between different pieces of wintertime folklore come from? We don't know for sure, but people have definitely been thinking about that.

For example, the "Shamanic Santa" theory was introduced by Carl Ruck, a professor from Boston University. It links the modern Santa myth to ancient shamanic practices from Siberian and Arctic cultures. Siberian reindeer herders (e.g., Evenki, Chukchi) practiced shamanism with mushroom use and reindeer central to their life and mythology.

Red and white suit? Colors of Amanita muscaria mushrooms. Flying reindeer? When reindeer consume Amanita, they exhibit strange behavior like jumping. Entering through chimney or roof? Shamans would enter snow-covered dwellings through roof openings. Gift giving? Shamans brought healing or visionary gifts from the spirit world. Sleigh flight? This could represent shamanic souls traveling or ecstatic journeying. Old man in charge? Shamans were seen as wise elders of their community.

These elements may have been introduced to Norse and Germanic traditions, then later evolved into Christian-era folklore (Saint Nicholas, Father Christmas), and eventually into Santa Claus.

This is only a theory. It is supported by some other scholars, but it is still questioned or dismissed by most mainstream historians and folklorists.

But mostly, anthropologists, historians, and folklorists agree that a much more basic logic lies beneath our stubborn consistency in having an old man be the face of midwinter celebrations.

Carl Jung (and later Joseph Campbell) discussed such figures as "Wise Old Men" archetypes, symbolizing death, transition, and transformation. And the winter solstice, being the symbolic death of the sun, naturally aligns with this archetype: end of the cycle (old man) must precede rebirth (new sun, new year).

These figures often represent a threshold, helping guide the world through the darkness of death into the light of rebirth.

And we seem to still feel it, deep down. This is not a matter of tradition or, to say precisely, not *only* a matter of tradition. Remember Ded Moroz? As I told you, this figure was invented by the Soviet government in the twentieth century—conjured up from some half-forgotten folklore. Not because they wanted to preserve tradition—not at all! What they wanted was the opposite: to break the tradition of Santa (because that's who was responsible for Christmas in the Russian Empire before the revolution). But the need was there: so deep, so obvious, that the government had to come up with a replacement quite similar to the original. Because the people want an old man in a long coat to come to us in the end of December and give us the gift of hope in the upcoming year.

Symbols of Yule (That We Know Very Well)

A holiday consists of little things: its colors, its smells, its special decorations. And when the holiday is no longer celebrated, its elements are often passed to the new one—just like with Yule and Christmas (or New Year, which in many countries is more important than Christmas).

These elements of Yule are well-known to us, so let's take a look at them and discover what they actually meant and what magic they brought to people in the past.

Fir Tree: All coniferous trees meant eternal life and immortality of the soul

Mistletoe: Healing, nourishing, care for the community

Holly: Protection, strength, victory over hardships of the winter

Green: The power of life, the promise of rebirth

Red: Vitality, merriment, strength

White: Snow, cleansing, beginning of a new cycle

Gold: The sun, light, the promise of better times

Wreaths and Round Baubles: Cycle of life and change of seasons (also, the sun!)

Fireplace: Ancestral support

Cinnamon and Other Spices: Protection against evil and misfortune

* * *

This is the magic we invoke every year to celebrate our favorite winter holidays. And I know that for many people, it really works as magic and helps them carry on with renewed hope and lifted spirits (and even combat seasonal depression).

> *Small Spell to Do on the Winter Solstice: Ice Melting Ritual*
>
> Freeze a small object, like a stone or charm, in a block of ice. Let it symbolize your wish, your inner spark, or happiness in your life. On the solstice, let it melt slowly by candlelight, symbolizing the thawing of darkness and the return of light.

The Magical Month of February

We might not see the last month of winter as especially wonderful or filled with ancient magic. But February was an important time even when it wasn't called February yet! Its various celebrations have roots deep enough to reach the Neolithic period (9500 BC).

Why? Because in the northern hemisphere, it marks the midpoint between the winter solstice and the spring equinox. It is the time of the very first signs of a new spring—and that carried a deep sacred meaning to people whose lives depended on nature reawakening.

In ancient Rome, February was named after the Latin term *februum*, which means "purification." A special ritual called Februa was hold on February 15. It was part of the festival of Lupercalia, associated with cleansing, fertility, and the god Faunus. Participants, often priests called *Luperci*, would sacrifice goats and a dog, then run through the streets striking people with strips of goat hide to bring fertility and purification.

Here we can see the main themes that will be obvious in other February celebrations from ancient Celtic Imbolc to our modern St. Valentine's Day.

Imbolc: The Festival of Crafts and Connections

Imbolc is a Celtic festival. Its name may be translated in several different ways:

- In the belly (goats and sheep are pregnant, just like the earth is pregnant with spring)
- In milk (cattle start lactating)
- Cleansing

The most important historical ritual of Imbolc is the Brigid's procession. People went out of their homes after the severe frosts of December and January and visited the neighboring villages to check on their relatives and friends. Some of them were expected to not have survived the dark Yule time, and there was a place for grief and funeral rites. But there was also a lot of feasting, merriment, and gift giving as well, because it was the time to celebrate reuniting with those who lived through the hardships.

During Imbolc festivities, people expressed deep love for each other, exchanged carefully crafted gifts, and discussed deals, partnerships, and marital engagements.

The goddess Brigid was honored on Imbolc and during the whole procession (around February 1 to 10). She represented crafts, blacksmiths, poetry and song, midwifery and healing, lambs and milk, birds, water and holy wells, and warfare. These areas of "expertise" might seem odd or random, but they were all highly relevant to the period of late winter and early spring.

Slavic February

In the Slavic folk calendar, February holds several interesting holidays.

Saint Trifon's day is still celebrated in Eastern and Southern Slavic countries on February 14. This is the day of banishing mice, blessing the grapevines, stargazing, and welcoming spring.

On February 15, *Gromnitsa* (Thunder Day) was celebrated. This day was dedicated to Perun: the god of sky, thunder and rain.

The next day, February 16, was also a holiday: *Kikimora*'s day (often referred to as kikimora's birthday). On that day, kikimora, a house spirit of ambiguous nature, needed to be appeased—if you did that, the year would be free of trouble, especially around the house.

And on February 21, *Vesnovey* (The Spring Winds) was celebrated. This is the day when spring was officially welcomed, and the house had to be cleaned, aired, and blessed.

The Themes of February

In all those holidays and celebrations, a set of themes can be easily noticed: cleansing and purification; love and connections; partnerships and contracts; and welcoming the first signs of spring.

And though we might not all celebrate Saint Trifon's day or Lupercalia today, we seem to still notice and revere the spirit of this special time. And of all the themes that the sacred month of February presents us with, we choose the one that is most dear to us: love.

St. Valentine's Day: Is It Magical?

There are two types of people: those who take St. Valentine's Day very seriously, and those who despise it as a shallow, commercial holiday which has nothing to do with actual love. The latter might be true in all respects but one: Long before Valentine's cards and mandatory bouquets, humans celebrated love, connections, and partnerships in February. They rejoiced at getting to see each other again, after a long and scary winter. They exchanged gifts they'd crafted for each other. They proposed engagements and welcomed new members to their families. They felt hopeful and encouraged by this new season, new spring, and new time of their lives starting.

I believe that this time was so saturated with meaning and magic, that even now we feel some piece of that ancient importance and urgency to honor love and the people around us. Magic or not, everyone decides for themselves. But, in a way, it definitely works.

> *Small Spell to Do on February 1:*
> *Miniature Sun Wands*
>
> Make tiny "sun wands" from cinnamon sticks and orange or yellow ribbons. Use them to bless your space with warm energy (and yes, pretending you are a fairy is allowed).

The Time of Eggs and Bunnies: What Do We Celebrate Around the Vernal Equinox?

For some people nowadays, Easter is a religious holiday, filled with sacred meaning. For others, this is more of a tradition: a merry time of bunnies and flowers, sweets and egg hunting... In this book, I'm going to refer to the latter: our modern-day spring celebration, which brings families fun and happy time together, even if they are not religious.

The Pagan Spring Celebration

Ostara is a pagan festival with deep roots in Celtic and Germanic traditions. It marked the beginning of spring—and of farming. The vernal equinox was an important astronomical point, dividing the seasons, just like the fall equinox and both solstices.

We all know the main symbols of Ostara since childhood, so let's look at their origins and meaning. You might be amazed how much we've taken directly from the ancient pagan times.

Easter Eggs

Eggs mean fertility and rebirth, even immortality; they represent the cyclical nature of life. Even today in some villages in Southern Slavic countries, people bury their dead with an egg so that they can be reborn, thanks to the power of life hidden in there.

Eggs are also connected with the sun, which can be hidden but also can be visible and shining—a bright yellow sphere surrounded by white light. (So, the tradition of hiding eggs and then looking for them is deeply symbolic!)

Pagans colored the eggs as a sign of gratitude and as offerings to the goddesses they honored during the spring equinox.

Bunnies

Rabbit and hare are both inseparable from Ostara, closely connected with spring, fertility, vitality, renewed joy, and with the moon, which rules over the waters, the herbs, and what was thought to be the female side of life.

Celtic and Germanic goddesses of spring often have rabbits as their companions: Ostara has two, one black and one white, and Olwen, a Welsh goddess of purity and renewal, has rabbits as white as clover flowers. Everywhere she goes, white flowers bloom.

So, our cute Easter bunnies were a part of the Vernal Equinox way before Easter itself existed.

Even the Easter Baskets!

Yes, they, too, go way back to the pagan celebration. The Norse goddesses Freyja and Frigg were honored on the day of the spring equinox. People brought them offerings, and those traditionally had to be brought in new baskets.

The Spring Resurrection

As we can see, all the decorative elements that are known to us have, in fact, been in use in the spring equinox rites since pre-Christian times. But what about the most important part of the holiday: its meaning? It seems that the whole idea of celebrating resurrection around this time is also ancient.

The sun restores its power on the day of the vernal equinox. Pagans have always celebrated its resurrection around this day. The Greek vegetation goddess Persephone comes back from the underworld to make her mother, Demeter, happy again; together they make the land bloom and bear fruit. Numerous solar gods come back from the dead: Mesopotamian Tammuz, Greek Adonis, Phrygian Attis...

So, when we partake in the Easter-time fun and its cheerful aesthetic, we actually follow the steps of ancient people, for whom all these elements, from eggs and bunnies to simple baskets, carried deep meaning and promised joy and jubilation. Getting to witness once more the return of the sun, of spring, carrying new promises and hopes—it still feels totally magical for many of us.

Small Spell to Do on the Vernal Equinox: Pocket Nest

Build a tiny nest from lint, threads, and twigs. Place it in your coat pocket or drawer. It invites comfort, small fortunes, and one fortunate coincidence.

Magical May Day: What Exactly Are We Celebrating on May 1?

There are mainly two May 1 celebrations nowadays: Labor Day or spring celebration. In many countries, including France, Germany, Italy, Russia, China, and others, May 1 is a public holiday.

In some cases, it is seen as a day to honor laborers and their rights. In others, it is the day when folk traditions of celebrating spring and welcoming summer are revived. For example, in some places in the UK, May Day still includes maypole dancing, Morris dancing, and crowning the May Queen.

In some places, these two faces of May 1 are combined. In Russia, this holiday is called the Day of Spring and Labor. It is a public holiday, and the strongest tradition is gathering in the countryside (or in the city parks) and having fun with friends or family by the fire (grilling meat is mandatory).

Ancient May Days

All of this can be easily traced back to ancient celebrations. Ancient Greek *Thargelia* in Athens were held around May 6 or 7 and honored Apollo and Artemis. The key themes were agricultural fertility, offering of the first fruits, and mighty protection rituals to avert plague and banish all evil. These traditions carried a strong message of "Everything better be well this season, because it is vitally important."

Ancient Roman *Floralia* were held on April 28 to May 3 and honored Flora, the goddess of flowers and spring. The traditions included theatrical performances, games, colorful clothing, scattering flower petals (especially roses), and the celebration of fertility, nature, and women's divinity.

In Germanic and Norse regions, the night of April 30 was sacred. This was the night when spirits and witches were believed to be active. Bonfires were lit to ward off evil spirits. Dancing and revelry took place, especially in the Harz Mountains of Germany. Later this festival was Christianized to honor Saint Walpurga, but the pagan roots of Walpurgisnacht have always remained.

And, of Course, Beltane

Beltane is a Celtic festival celebrated on May 1. It celebrates the beginning of summer and opens the season of the most active farmwork (a Labor Day, too, in a way). This is the midpoint between the spring equinox and the summer solstice.

The first mention of Beltane was made in an Irish text dating back to the tenth century. The original name of Beltane is, by some scholars, thought to be *bellotania*—"the bright fires." Beltane is traditionally a festival honoring goddesses (just like ancient Roman Floralia!), but one particular god is also connected with it. It's Belenos, a solar deity who travels the sky in a chariot made of pure sunlight. He is always journeying and is sometimes called "the beautiful exile."

Beltane is a festival opposing Samhain on the wheel of the year. They have one specific thing in common: rituals addressing ancestors. On Beltane, two grand bonfires were lit, and people led their cattle between them as a ritual of purification and requested blessings from ancestors.

Beltane is also a classic time for protection spells. It is an ancient Beltane tradition to put shiny things on trees growing at the edge of the forest. It distracted the fairy folk so they hopefully forgot to come to the village and mess with people.

And, of course, Beltane is known for being a time for love and fertility magic. Fun fact: According to medieval records, more people were born in February than in any other month. And that means: *Beltane children*.

As we can see, Beltane (as well as other ancient May Day festivals) is centered around love, passion, fertility, creating future abundance, connecting with ancestors, warding off envy and evil, fearless self-expression, dreaming big, setting ambitious goals, and, ultimately, letting our wild nature shine like a bright bonfire.

And those who still gather around the fire in nature with their friends, some great food, and good stories—or dance around the maypole and choose a May Queen—keep this wild, bright magic alive. Even if all they meant to do is have some fun.

Small Spell to Do on May 1:
Lantern of Secret Blooming

Take a lantern or jar and fill it with herbs, petals, and glowing objects (fairy lights, glow sticks, crystals). Whisper into it something that is beginning to grow in you—new love, courage, weirdness, etc. Place it outside overnight to commune with May Day spirits.

Midsummer's Half-Forgotten Magic

Strangely enough, celebrating the summer solstice isn't such a big thing now in most parts of the world. We don't have big modern holidays that follow the steps of the pagan Midsummer—as modern winter holidays like Christmas or New Year's do for the winter solstice. There are some countries where Midsummer is still an important holiday—mostly in Northern and Central Europe.

In Sweden, for example, this day is second only to Christmas. People gather on the closest Friday or Saturday to June 24 (St. John's Day, which stepped in to take the summer solstice's place in Christian times).

They dance around the maypole (yes, in June) wearing flower crowns, singing traditional songs, and eating pickled herring, new potatoes, and strawberries. I've been to such Midsommar celebrations in a small town called Sigtuna, and it felt like the past came to life, effortlessly and naturally.

Other countries where Midsummer is still revered include Finland, Estonia, Latvia, Lithuania, Norway, Denmark, and Iceland.

Litha: The Celtic Midsummer

Witches, pagans, and fans of Celtic culture celebrate *Litha* on the day of the summer solstice. It is a grand event, a counterpart to Yule. Its symbolism combines light and darkness, which makes this festival a little bit spooky.

The summer solstice is the point from which days start getting shorter, and that means that while, yes, it's a light and sunny festival, it is also the exact day when darkness begins to creep back in. Remember the two kings that fight on Yule night? They meet in battle again on Litha, and this time the victory goes to the Holly King, who embodies darkness, night, and death.

Midsummer is the time when the fae folk are in their highest power. Fairies are beautiful beings, but they were also traditionally considered dangerous. (Today, most practitioners and believers in magic agree that you just shouldn't mock them, make foolish deals with them, or leave trash in nature, and you'll be fine.)

Many stories of people who carelessly wandered into the fairy realm and paid for their curiosity are said to have taken place on Midsummer: most often, around midday or midnight.

Not only fairies, but all nature spirits were thought to become really strong during the summer solstice. This wasn't exclusive for Celtic Litha; for example, forest guardian spirits like *Leshy* in Slavic cultures got especially restless during the Ivan Kupala's night (St. John's, just like in the Central Europe). It was by far the worst possible time to get lost in the woods.

The Plant Lore of Midsummer

Plants and herbs were collected during Midsummer. For many modern herbalists, this is still the way things are done: Several important medicinal herbs reach their fullest potential at this time of year. Summer feels naturally connected with plants, but this connection was more than just logic for ancient people. They believed that herbs actually become magical once a year on the summer solstice.

For example, St. John's Wort is widely collected and dried for protection around Midsummer. It really helps to boost mood and energy level if you infuse and drink it—a proven fact.

According to other legends, five herbs gain magical power on the night of Midsummer. The already mentioned St. John's Wort could cleanse and heal. Clover brought luck. Rue protected from all evil. Rose granted beauty and youth. And verbena could even give you a witch's power and influence over the unseen world.

* * *

Slavic legends say that on Ivan Kupala's night the fern flower (a rare and magical talisman) can be found. Magical properties of the fern flower were impressive: it was thought to grant any wishes, help find treasure, unlock any locks, make your love interest fall in love with you, heal all wounds and diseases, grant wisdom and spiritual purity, give clairvoyance and power over spirits, and, last but not least, make you invisible when you needed it!

The instructions on how to look for the fern flower on the Midsummer night were numerous, but quite clear. You ought to go looking in solitude, in silence, and at midnight sharp (the fern was believed to bloom only for a moment). You couldn't take any light with you. You had to be ready to fight the dark forces protecting the flower (and if you got distracted by them, they would tear you apart). Once you pick the flower, you should keep it safe and always carry with you.

* * *

Break-open-herb (*razryv-trava*) has a similar, but slightly different legend. Its main magical property is to open any locks and break down anything made of iron.

Its other names included *klin-trava*, *skakun-trava* (jump-herb), *raskounik*, *razkovniche*, *rozryw*, etc.

In many regions, people believed that red clover was that mythical break-open-herb. So, the idea of lucky clover is connected with the break-open-herb and fern flower! (It would be appropriate to guess that finding a four-leaf clover on the summer solstice is an absolute win, giving you ultimate luck.)

But how did one find a break-open-herb on this magical night? Luckily, there were multiple ways. You could come across it accidentally: A scythe will break if it hits the herb and a horse will lose its shoes if it steps on it. Or you could collect some herbs and throw them into a river or a stream and watch. Only the magical break-open-herb will float against the current. But if you are in Serbia, only a hedgehog can help you! Take it with you and it'll show you the way to the razryv-trava. In other countries, different chthonic animals, like grass snakes, helped.

* * *

Many, many more legends say that plants could become literally magical during this high summertime. The roots of these beliefs are ancient. And we still meet an echo of this old plant magic here and there, be it dancing in flower wreaths around the maypole, picking a floral print dress for a warm summer day, or brewing cold tea with fresh mint and rosemary in the sunshine.

> *Small Spell to Do on the Summer Solstice: Dandelion Crown for the Sun*
>
> Make a crown of dandelions and place it on a rock, a fence post, or a tree stump. Say, "This is for the sun, who gives and takes."

Subtle and Sacred: August, Celebrated

Country fairs, agricultural festivals, the traditional days of honey, apples, and bread… All this happens in August, but it feels so natural that we don't usually think of them as some old pagan tradition; it's just the way things are. But the whole essence of these customs lies in ancient agricultural magic: to honor, bless, and multiply the crops. Subtly, these rituals crept into modern times, bringing us fun and wholesome pastimes. So, what treats does ancient August's magic offer, and what were all those fairs and harvest festivals really about?

Lughnasadh: Remembering the Old Traditions

Modern-day pagans, witches, and Celtic culture enthusiasts know about *Lughnasadh*. This festival has its own Christianized version, just like Samhain and Yule: It's called Lammas or Loaf Mass. However, most people don't seem to need a holiday at the beginning of August: neither Lughnasadh nor Lammas are present in modern popular culture. They've been replaced by the traditional fairs and markets I mentioned earlier. But sometimes, the name and the date of the holiday are forgotten, while traditional celebrations stay intact. Let me show you how we still celebrate Lughnasadh and similar seasonal holidays, even though we are rarely aware of it.

For ancient Celts, Lughnasadh was a symbolic triumph of the material world: wealth, health, nature's abundance, and beauty. Originally celebrated on the closest full moon to the beginning of August, it was dedicated to the beginning of harvesting and to the first crops. And, of course, to the god Lugh. By the way, Lugh was highly influential: the towns Lyon, London, Lugano, and Loudun were named after him.

He was the god of light, skill, craftsmanship, and leadership. He was often called Lugh Lámhfhada ("Lugh of the Long Arm") and was considered a master of all arts—poetry, smithing, war, music, magic, and more.

And his festival reflected all of his traits and domains.

Harvesting and Farmers' Markets

Lughnasadh was the festival of the first crops; the first fruits of the year were brought together on public display to honor them, to trade them, and, partly, just to show them to the community.

In this, we easily recognize modern-day farmers' markets and fairs, where fellowship and trading are still present, along with deep respect for the earth's gifts.

Contests, Games, and More Hard Work

Lughnasadh is called a harvest festival, but that's not the whole truth. It marks the *beginning* of harvesting, and the main focus is not gratitude and abundance, but rather the forthcoming hard farmwork (the time for gratitude and celebrating abundance will come in September, on the autumnal equinox).

On Lughnasadh, ancient Celts held competitions and games. The contests were numerous but could be divided into two categories. Martial and athletic competitions: foot races, wrestling, boxing, spear and javelin throwing, stone lifting, horse races, and chariot races. These were tests of strength, endurance, and skill, often similar in spirit to the ancient Greek Olympics.

And then there were cultural contests: poetry recitations, storytelling, singing, musical performances, riddle and wit contests. Such events showcased bardic talent, which was highly respected in Celtic society.

The winners earned...the right to work harder than all the others, organizing the festive feast and subsequent harvesting work! Yes, the winners gladly worked more than the others—such is the lesson of Lughnasadh.

We still enjoy contests and win prizes during August country fairs—even though the winners don't get that much responsibility now.

Slavic Harvest Festivals: The Three August Spas

In parts of Russia, Ukraine, and Belarus, August is marked by three traditional holidays known as the Spas: Honey Spas (August 14), Apple Spas (August 19), and Nut or Bread Spas (August 29). Though now framed within Orthodox Christianity, these festivals preserve deep-rooted pre-Christian harvest traditions and remain widely celebrated, especially in rural areas.

Each Spas reflects a key stage in the agricultural calendar. Honey Spas begins the Dormition Fast and celebrates the first honey harvest, with honey and herbs brought to church for blessing. Apple Spas, the most popular, coincides with the Feast of the Transfiguration and marks the moment when apples may be eaten and shared—symbolizing the fruitfulness of the land. Nut Spas, the final in the series, honors the grain and nut harvests and often includes the blessing of freshly baked bread.

These holidays blend folk ritual, seasonal change, and religious observance, serving as a living bridge between ancient agrarian culture and modern-day spirituality. Despite centuries of transformation, the Spas continue to bring communities together in celebration of nature's abundance—and we can still feel the same reverence toward nature's gifts that ancient people did many centuries ago.

Small Spell to Do on August 1: Wild Game Night
Play a silly competition with friends—stone skipping, wheelbarrow racing, cheese-wheel rolling. Crown the winner with herbs.

Autumnal Equinox: The Season of Pumpkin Spice Latte?

We sure celebrate the vernal equinox today in the form of Easter. But do we have similar traditions for its counterpart, the autumnal equinox? It happens at the end of September, somewhere between September 20 and 23.

In China, Vietnam, and Korea, there is a mid-autumn festival close to the equinox. In Japan, the holiday of *Shūbun no Hi* is celebrated with visiting ancestors' graves and appreciating seasonal beauty. In the rural communities of Northern Europe, local harvest festivals occur around this time. But no big, universally known holiday is held on the autumnal equinox nowadays.

Still, a deep look at some seasonal patterns in our lives suggests that we all still celebrate this cosmic event every year. We just do it casually, low-key, and for a long period of time. And this is especially clear when we examine the phenomenon of the "fall aesthetic."

Each September, all these things happen, surely as the equinox itself… Social media blows up with cozy fall lifestyle content. People rewatch their favorite "fall shows" and "fall movies" with almost religious devotion (for many, it's *Gilmore Girls* and *Twilight*). The cafes and shops decorate their windows with yellow leaves and pumpkins (seasonal decorations may seem trivial, but the same businesses very rarely do that, say, when summer arrives). And, of course, the seasonal fall drinks reemerge in most coffee shops with the pumpkin spice latte being the most popular, but far from the only one.

We vigorously celebrate and welcome the fall season, even though now we usually don't have a special holiday to do this on. But that wasn't always the case…

Celtic Mabon: An Ancient Festival or a New Age Fake?

In quite a lot of neo-pagan and modern witchcraft traditions, the autumnal equinox is called *Mabon*. But it is the only seasonal festival of the wheel of the year concept that doesn't have a historic Celtic name.

So, when witches and pagans of the twentieth century were putting traditions of the wheel of the year together, they had to give this festival a name. And now the autumnal equinox is called Mabon. But where does it come from? And does that mean that Mabon is a fake?

The name Mabon was derived from a Celtic god's name, Maponos. Also, several inscriptions were found, mentioning *Mabon ab Modron* ("Divine son of the Divine Mother"). Then, there is a Welsh legend of Culhwch and Olwen, where Mabon is mentioned. The legend itself is medieval, but it might have much more ancient origins.

Celts didn't call the autumnal equinox Mabon—but did they celebrate it? There were no outdoor fire festivals and feasts, and that makes some people think that there was no celebration at all. But that's not true.

* * *

The autumnal equinox was celebrated in many cultures around the world (don't worry, we'll get back to the Celts soon). In ancient

Greece, the autumnal equinox was dedicated to Persephone who returned to the underworld each year around this time. In ancient Rome, it was the day to honor the goddess Pomona as well as the festival of grapes and wine. Even Christians celebrated the autumnal equinox in a way: this day is dedicated to the Archangel Michael.

* * *

The ancient Celts celebrated the autumnal equinox as well, not with massive festivals and feasts, but as a family holiday and a day to thank the gods for the crops.

The gratitude rituals were carried out only if the year's harvest was successful. The families discussed their needs and requests and made their plans for the colder season. It was a calm and cozy holiday, with a tradition of welcoming guests and visiting neighbors' homes. Apples were a traditional food for the celebration, as a symbol of life and death and of being at the border of two seasons. Druids performed gratitude rituals for the trees, but they did it privately, without audience.

So, Mabon is a valid ancient festival. It's not a noisy and showy one, but it has deep meaning…and a new name.

Small Spell to Do on the Autumnal Equinox: Mushroom Wish Walk

Spot the first mushroom of the day. Close your eyes, think of something you're longing for, and step over it without looking back.

Chapter 5

Household Magic

*How your home is a living altar:
ancestors on mantels, mirrors as portals, and more.*

There is an old kind of magic that lives in our homes. It's not always loud or ceremonial. Most of the time, we don't even notice it. It hides in the everyday: the way we light a candle in the evening, arrange flowers on a table, or place family photos above the fireplace. We say we're decorating, making things cozy, keeping a tradition. But something older is moving beneath the surface.

Long before electricity or modern floor plans, the home was a sacred place, every part of it carrying deep symbolic meaning. Fireplaces were hearth-altars. Mirrors were portals to the spirit world. The front door was a threshold not only to the street, but to other worlds, which were not always kind. Even now, our homes quietly remember some of this.

We no longer think of ourselves as performing rituals. Yet we repeat ancient gestures daily. We may take off our shoes at the door (a rite of purification), hang protective symbols without knowing their roots, and fill our space with items that hold memory and intention. The old ways have stayed, but our way of thinking about them has changed (and keeps changing, from generation to generation).

This chapter is a walkthrough of the rooms of your home, looking again at the familiar through the eyes of history, magic, and folk traditions. Not to make it look strange and exotic—but to recognize what has been there all along.

At the Threshold: Protecting and Inviting at the Door

The entrance to a home is more than just a way in. It's a threshold between the outer world and the intimate world of the household. In folk traditions across the globe, the front door is a powerful boundary—a place where energies are filtered, where the unwanted are kept out, and the welcome are called in.

To this day, people decorate their doors. Sometimes it's seasonal—a wreath in winter, a bouquet in spring. Sometimes it's more permanent—a horseshoe nailed above the door, a string of bells, a small bundle of herbs or pine tucked into the frame. Ornaments were originally not decorative in nature but instead were charms of protection or invitation. A horseshoe turned upward caught good luck and held it. Bells frightened away wandering spirits. Green branches, especially from plants like juniper or rowan, were guardians against the evil eye. And wreaths, as you already know from the previous chapter, are symbols of the sun, of rebirth, and of the cyclical nature of all things in the world. A wreath on the front door is basically saying: "Let things go their way, and everything in this house will be as it should."

Even the act of wiping one's feet or removing shoes before entering holds special meaning. Yes, it is about cleanliness—but also, it's a ritual of leaving behind the dust of the road, the worries and pain (and even malicious spirits!) that might cling to you. In Russia, to step into someone's home without taking off your shoes is more than rude—this is a consistent from villages to cities. It's a breach of the home's sacred space, a violation of the invisible boundary that marks the house as a place of safety, warmth, and respect.

Crossing the threshold has always been a quiet kind of magic—one we still perform, even if we no longer have the words for it.

The Window

Windows are the home's organs of vision and breath, and they are an invitation of a kind: people can glimpse through, the fresh air flows in... It is a transparent veil where domestic magic meets the outer breath of wind and sky (along with myriads unseen spirits). In the folklore of many regions, the window is a spiritual lung: It exhales warmth and stories, and it inhales omens, dreams, and news of the unseen. Perhaps this is why, across so many cultures, windows were always dressed and adorned, much like people.

In premodern Europe, especially in Northern and Eastern traditions, windows were decorated seasonally, ritually, and purposefully. The patterns traced in frost, the embroidery of lace curtains, the hand-cut silhouettes of paper, even the placement of certain symbols—crosses, circles, runes—formed a subtle language. They could carry different messages: some to neighbors, some to spirits, some to the dead. A star-shaped ornament hanging in the center of the window could be a sign of hope, of protection, or of the returning sun. In Slavic homes, garlands of herbs or flowers might be draped across the sill not only to scent the room but to invite the *domovoi* (a helpful household spirit) to come near the windows more often and ward off the jealous glance of some unclean force.

And always—candles. To place a candle in the window is one of the oldest forms of home magic. (And it feels so good, doesn't it?) In medieval Ireland and Scotland, it was a signal to travelers, human or otherwise, that this was a place of warmth and shelter. On holy nights, candles burned not only for the living but to welcome the souls of the dead back for brief visits. In parts of Eastern Europe, especially around the solstices, candles in the windows served as guiding lights for the spirits of ancestors, a quiet form of hospitality for the invisible.

Even the plants chosen for window ledges have long-lost meanings. Geraniums, now the humble companion of suburban windowsills, were once believed to protect against all that is evil and unholy. Their pungent scent was thought to displease demons. Basil, sacred to both Mediterranean witches and Orthodox priests, invited love and sanctity (and was used to sprinkle the holy water while blessing the house). Rosemary by the window was a charm for memory, clarity, and protection—a living prayer. Ivy, trained along the pane, whispered loyalty and quiet strength. In ancient Rome, windows with potted violets or roses might indicate the dwelling of someone engaged in priestly rites or private cults, while in medieval Germany, marigolds and rue were planted to keep witches at bay or, more likely, to pacify and please the passing souls of witches who flew by night.

In truth, windows were dressed so lavishly in many old traditions because they were considered a liminal point, a place of encounter between the house and the street, between the family and the wandering dead, between the intimate world and the impersonal, often harsh, seasons. What was placed there—be it a candle, an ornament, or a message stitched into lace—was part declaration, part defense, part invitation. It was never meant solely for those who lived inside, because the window was always seen as a place for dialogue. Decorative and magical items were used as words in this conversation.

Mantlepiece Magic: The Hearth, the Stove, and the Spirits of the Ancestors

Everyone knows the story of Cinderella. Her name reflects the fact that she was always covered in cinders or ash. "Cinderella" isn't her only name, nor is it the only version of this tale. She has many names—Zolushka, Papaluga—all derived from the word for ash in various languages.

There's also the well-known Russian folktale of Yemelya, who lay for years on his home's stove until he set off on an adventure… riding the stove, which, at his magical command, began to move. In some versions of the story, the hero is even born from the stove itself.

The stove or hearth appears in fairy tales as a place close to magic, often helping the hero or heroine. This is not by accident; it carried echoes of real cultic and domestic practices from ancient times. As Vladimir Propp writes in his essay "Folklore and Reality," the hearth was symbolically tied to ancestor worship. Across cultures, people believed that "the spirit of the ancestor lived in the hearth." The heroes of folktales carry the memory of this belief. By being "born" from the hearth, they reenact the return or rebirth of a strong ancestor within the family line.

Among some Indigenous peoples of North America, it is believed that on the Day of the Dead, the spirits of the departed rise from beneath the hearth—from the hollow where ashes gather. After emerging, they proceed to a meal prepared especially for them. In many cultures, when families moved from one place to another, they would carry ashes with them so that the household spirit—the guardian of the home—could move too. Household spirits, often seen as later versions of ancestral spirits, appear in every culture where the hearth holds a central place.

Exactly how the hearth was connected to the ancestor cult is a subject of scholarly debate. On the one hand, we have clear archaeological evidence of burials inside homes. Most of these remains are children's—likely buried indoors to ensure their souls would return and be reborn in the family. However, Propp notes that, once people settled in permanent homes, this practice became impractical—there simply wasn't enough space. But in semi-nomadic cultures, the practice was common and convenient: When it came time to move, people would leave behind their old dwellings (and the graves within them) and begin anew. In such societies, the dead always had room.

However, at that stage in cultural development, the hearth wasn't yet inside the home. There was a communal fire—large, central, and constantly maintained. This fire itself was sacred and deeply linked to the ancestors. Its burning was kept up continuously, just as the family line continued without interruption—one generation entering the realm of the dead as another was born, perhaps with the spirit of an ancestor.

Propp suggests that in settled agricultural societies, the cult of fire and the cult of ancestors merged—not in practice (since burials within the home had ceased), but in consciousness. By then, fire had entered the house and retained its sacred status, while the dead (with occasional exceptions) had departed from the physical home but remained in memory, in stories, and in practice. The hearth came to hold a double meaning: It was both a place of power and a dwelling of the ancestors.

Many other scholars argue for a more direct link between the hearth and ancestor worship. But even if we take Propp's more cautious interpretation, the point remains: Since deep antiquity, people have imagined their ancestors living in or near the hearth. This is reflected in both archaeology and culture—including those fairy tales about ash-covered heroes and heroines who sit by the fire at home and, in the end, receive magical help and a happy ending.

* * *

Now let's turn to the modern home. If there's a fireplace, chances are there are family photographs on the mantel. There we find both the living and the departed—an entire lineage or the most beloved representatives of it. Sometimes, there's even an urn with ashes placed there. Why do people do this? Because it's tradition. Because it makes sense. Because it feels right.

But the overlap between this intuitive, modern gesture and the essence of ancient belief is clear and striking. This literal continuation of the ancestral cult—combined with the complete loss of memory about *why* we do it—is a remarkable and vivid example of how ancient beliefs and magic persist in our lives, even after their original meanings have faded from memory.

Fire Witchcraft or Cozy Atmosphere? Candles as the Simplest House Magic

Not every home has a fireplace, but almost everyone lights candles from time to time. Some do it only on birthdays or when the power goes out. But most people don't limit candle lighting to those occasions—otherwise, candles wouldn't be so popular and omnipresent in home goods stores or among clothing and cosmetics brands.

It's important to note that even in the most ordinary, modern usage, a candle is never lit for no reason. It's done, for example, to mark the boundary between "ordinary" time—when we focus on chores, work, and daily routine—and "time for ourselves," moments of relaxation, pleasure, rest, or a special dinner with family or friends. Lighting a candle sends a clear mental signal: "Now something pleasant is about to happen; this is a gift for me or my loved ones." Different people mark different events with candle lighting—usually their favorite ones, the moments they value most. So in one home, candles come out for a lavish dinner party with friends, and in another, for meditation, a soothing bath, or watching a favorite TV show.

A candle gives cozy, soft light, but that's not the only reason for its popularity: after all, there are equally cozy nightlights and other forms of localized lighting. I believe we still carry a sacred awe of fire, a special relationship with this element. Fire has been vital to humanity since time immemorial.

Ancient communities never did rituals, sacrifices, or communal meals—where stories were shared, songs sung, and dances danced—without fire. Fire meant safety, warmth, plenty, and the closeness of one's tribe, as well as the closeness of ancestral spirits and gods.

For example, the ancient Zoroastrians of Persia practiced one of the oldest known fire cults, tending an eternal flame as a symbol of divine purity and cosmic order. In Celtic traditions, sacred fires were kindled during seasonal festivals like Beltane and were believed to protect the community and promote fertility. Among the Vedic peoples of ancient India, fire rituals (*yajnas*) formed the core of religious practice, with fire acting as a mediator between humans and the gods.

No matter the culture, fire symbolically represented the intersection of the strongest magic with everyday comfort and well-being. That's how we still perceive it today, even if unconsciously.

Moreover, the widespread availability of candles for the home has become a huge help for "closeted witches"—those who feel drawn to magical practice but aren't ready to do it openly in their family homes for fear of judgment. Buying a scented candle at a home goods store, making a wish (or maybe even carving a symbol into the wax with a needle when no one is watching), then lighting it "just for the atmosphere" is something many secret witches do. And I'm very glad that today's "domestic fire cult" gives them this opportunity.

Your Own Domestic Portal: Mirror Magic We All Do

Mirrors have always held a strange kind of power in our homes. We glance into them every day—mostly mindlessly, but sometimes in search of something more than just our reflections. And even now, when most people don't consider themselves superstitious, mirror-related customs continue quietly in the background of daily life.

In many homes, mirrors are covered when someone dies. This custom is found in Jewish tradition, but also appears widely across Eastern Europe, Germany, Italy, and the American South. The belief is that a soul, newly released, might get confused and become trapped in the reflective surface or even pulled back into the world through it. In some households, especially older ones, this is still instinctively done—mirrors are draped with scarves or bedsheets, as if to let the air settle and the spirit pass on gently.

In some rural Balkan households, mirrors were covered not only for mourning, but also during storms or childbirth—times when the veil between worlds was thinner and demanded caution. This, too, lingers: There's still something about a mirror at night, when the house is silent and lit only by a small lamp, that feels unsettling. Some people turn them around or move them away without knowing quite why.

Another persistent tradition is not placing mirrors directly across from beds. The explanation given today might be practical ("I don't want to see my reflection at night and get startled"), but in many cultures, it was believed that mirrors draw in energy—and could even steal your soul while you sleep. In feng shui, a mirror facing the bed is still said to disturb rest and invite conflict.

Even the idea of checking your appearance before leaving the house—so common it feels like instinct—may carry older echoes. In Slavic folk belief, a quick glance into the mirror before stepping outside was a way to affix your soul to your body, helping you keep wholeness and luck intact in public spaces. In some regions, children were gently encouraged to smile into a mirror before leaving home, so that the "image left behind" would protect them.

Breaking a mirror still brings anxiety. Even people who laugh it off often pause for a moment, uneasy. The superstition about seven years of bad luck comes from Roman times: They believed life renewed every seven years, and that mirrors reflected not just the body, but the soul's current state. Breaking one could impact your fate.

There's also the tradition of mirrors in entryways—a practice that thrives today. Designers say it's for light and aesthetics. But folk tradition says otherwise: A mirror by the door protects the household, bouncing back any harmful intent a guest might bring with them. This is especially potent if the mirror reflects the front door itself, "sending back" negativity before it ever crosses the threshold.

Finally, think about hand mirrors. Once ornamental and carried like talismans, they were not just for checking one's beauty, but for protection. In many cultures, they could ward off the evil eye—some Slavic and Mediterranean brides still carry small mirrors in their bouquets or shoes to confuse jealous spirits. And in Slavic folk tales, such mirrors are often gifts from supernatural helpers, which can distract the evil pursuers and save the protagonists' lives. Today's compact mirrors might seem far from magic, but perhaps they still carry a hint of symbolic shielding.

So much of mirror lore survives not as formal belief, but as gesture, design, discomfort, or habit. We cover them, avoid certain placements, keep them near our doors, and regret breaking them. Even when we tell ourselves it's just about style or convenience, the old magic shines faintly behind the glass...as if it's watching us, just as we watch ourselves.

The Small Things We Keep: Figurines, Tokens, and Ancient Totems

Some objects in our homes feel more important than they should. A porcelain dog on the shelf. A little wooden owl by the books. A collection of ceramic frogs on the kitchen windowsill. A pair of elephants facing the doorway. A tiny horse on the mantel. We rarely ask why they're there. They just are. They've been with us for years, maybe decades. Some were gifts, others were things we picked up "just because"—but we don't want to part with them.

These small pieces of home decor may look like innocent trinkets, but their roots run deep in the ancient world of totems and protective spirits. Across countless cultures, people once believed that each clan or family had a totem animal—a sacred companion, guardian, or ancestor who watched over them. It was honored in carvings, sculptures, clothing, and even household placement.

And even after totemism faded from formal belief systems, its logic survived—especially in the home.

Many of the most common "decorative" animals today were once thought to bring good luck or ward off harm. Frogs, for instance, were seen as symbols of rebirth and fertility in Ancient Egypt and later as protectors of the home in Slavic and Balkan traditions. Cats—particularly black ones—were both feared and revered, seen as witches' familiars but also household guardians. Horses brought strength, freedom, and prosperity; owls, wisdom and foresight; elephants, longevity and spiritual memory.

Elephants with their trunks up, in particular, are considered lucky in both South and Southeast Asian traditions, and this belief spread worldwide. You'll still find them on side tables, bookcases, and entryway stands. Some people insist they must face the door to draw blessings in.

Dogs, both as live companions and figurines, have long been thought to protect the home. In ancient Rome, mosaics at the entrance of homes often depicted barking dogs with the phrase *cave canem* ("beware of the dog"), not just as warnings to intruders, but as symbolic guardians as well. Today, many homes feature small dog statues or photos by the door—part decoration, part quiet watchman.

Even decorative birds carry layers of meaning on their wings. Swallows were once painted above hearths to bring the household safely through the year. Roosters stood as protectors against evil spirits. In many cultures, a rooster figurine in the kitchen or dining area is still believed to keep the home lively and safe.

Collections are especially telling. The impulse to gather many versions of the same animal—owls, elephants, foxes—often goes unexplained. It feels natural in a way. But in earlier times, having multiple images of a totem animal strengthened its presence. It was a way to invite that power into the home again and again.

Isn't it remarkable that we still surround ourselves with these artificial creatures and feel comforted by their quiet company? Whether or not we believe in their power, we still give them the honored role of guardians and vessels of special powers.

The Scented Veil: Perfume, Memory, and Home Enchantment

Scents are everywhere now. Candles, essential oil diffusers, incense sticks, wax melts, room sprays, fresheners hidden in wardrobes or drawers… Most people today don't use them to mask odors alone, but to create a certain mood. A touch of lavender to relax. Orange and cinnamon to feel festive. Vanilla for comfort. It's personal and instinctive—but also ancient.

Scent has always been, and still is, used in rituals: It's a powerful tool of transformation. In early cultures, specific smells were thought to shift the space itself and even draw unseen beings—spirits, gods, ancestors—closer. It feels logical in a way; smells are unseen, but potent and unmistakably there. Just like spirits and other supernatural beings! Perhaps they are made of similar stuff…

Frankincense and myrrh were used in Egyptian, Babylonian, and early Christian rituals. These resins, when burned, created thick, slow smoke that carried prayers upward and purified the space.

Frankincense was thought to lift the soul, while myrrh grounded and protected it. They were often used together in temples and tombs alike.

In ancient Greece and Rome, thyme was burned to sharpen the mind and give courage. Its name comes from the Greek *thymos*, meaning spirit or breath. Warriors bathed in thyme-scented water before battle, and homes were cleansed with it in the spring.

Lavender was beloved across medieval Europe not only for its clean, floral scent but also as a protection charm. People hung it over doorways and tucked it into bedsheets to guard against evil, sickness, and nightmares. To this day, it remains a scent associated with rest and healing.

Sandalwood was—and still is—sacred in Hindu and Buddhist practices. Used in prayer beads, incense, and oils, its gentle, woody aroma calms the mind and invites meditation. It is said to guide wandering thoughts back toward the center.

Citrus peels, especially orange, were traditionally dried and burned in Chinese and Mediterranean households to refresh energy and attract abundance. Orange oil was considered especially lucky for the new year. Today, citrus scents are still linked to energy, optimism, and overall wholesomeness and cheer.

So, when we choose scents for our home today—floral, spicy, smoky, or woody—we're doing what humans have always done: using fragrance to shape mood, mark space, and invite a subtle kind of magic into our daily lives. The only thing that's changed is the packaging...and probably the degree of seriousness around the whole process.

Bouquets and Offerings: The Silent Speech of Flowers

A vase of flowers may seem like one of the simplest, most innocent household decorations—but it once served as an offering or even a sacrifice. Placing fresh flowers inside the home was a way of honoring invisible presences like house spirits, ancestors, and gods; the bouquet was not as much for us, as for them.

In Slavic folk tradition, flowers were a form of communication with the domovoi. A small bunch of wildflowers placed by the hearth or in the sacred "red" corner was meant to show respect and hospitality to the spirit of the home. In some rural regions of Russia and Ukraine, it was still common well into the twentieth century to place flowers on windowsills "so the dead would not be lonely." The belief was that the ancestors still passed through the house and could read the messages sent by particular flowers.

In ancient Greece, cut flowers were part of offerings to household gods and the dead. White lilies, myrtle, and violets were favored for their scent and purity, while poppies and asphodels were linked to the underworld. Asphodel in particular was planted by graves, placed in vases, and even woven into garlands meant to soothe the souls of the departed.

The Victorian "language of flowers," though often romanticized now as a secret code for courtship, had much older roots. It drew from Ottoman Turkish *selam* traditions, where specific flowers and herbs conveyed entire messages. A sprig of rosemary meant remembrance. A marigold, sorrow. Lavender could mean trust or silence. Many of these symbols crossed into the world of mourning customs. For example, in nineteenth-century England, mourners placed ivy in the home to honor the dead and to let the spirits know they were remembered and welcomed.

Japanese *ikebana*—the ritual art of flower arranging—originated as an offering to spirits at household altars. The practice emphasized mindfulness and presence. The vertical line of a single branch was meant to connect earth and heaven. Today, this art is practiced on memorial days and for festivals for the dead.

A vase of flowers can transform a room. But perhaps it also reminds something unseen that it hasn't been forgotten.

Magic Underfoot: Carpets as Protection, Blessing, and Spellwork

Long before carpets became mere decoration or a comfort underfoot, they were powerful tools of household magic. Woven by hand, thread by thread, they embodied the logic of the cosmos, offering protection, blessing, fertility, and control over space. A carpet was in fact a lot of things: a map of the world, a shield from evil, a threshold, and sometimes even a prayer.

The idea of "covering" the ground was always a magical one at its core. In many early cultures—especially among the nomadic peoples of Central Asia and the Middle East—the earth was sacred, but also unpredictable. Spirits were believed to dwell beneath the surface. A carpet acted as a protective barrier between the people and the underworld and between the human household and the raw, untamed world outside. The boundary mattered. You could invite in what you wanted—blessing, abundance, health, warmth—and keep out what you feared.

Patterns, too, were never chosen at random. Every motif had a function. The ram's horn pattern, most common in Turkish and Caucasian rugs, stood for strength and virility and blessed a house with vitality and protection. The *elibelinde* or "hands on hips" motif represented a goddess figure—a symbol of fertility and the feminine. The eye or *nazar* motif, always watchful, was meant to deflect the evil eye and bring luck. Stars and crosses were not only celestial—they protected doorways and sacred corners.

Borders mattered deeply. They weren't just framing devices, but actual magical fences. A strong, clear border was thought to "contain" the blessing inside the carpet and keep harmful forces from entering. A home rug with broken or open borders might be beautiful—but it also might be dangerous.

Color, too, had power. Red—dominant in many Central Asian and Middle Eastern rugs—was the color of life, fire, and protection. Blue calmed and purified, suggesting other worlds and their help. Green invoked growth and divine blessings but also transition and change. Black could be used for boundaries, mourning, or to trap bad energy.

In traditional settings, a carpet marked sacred space. In many cultures, prayers are performed on rugs, because the rug itself defines and blesses the space. A guest would be invited to sit on the best rug as a sign of honor and true hospitality. A bride might step onto a special wedding rug to bless the new marriage. A newborn might be laid on a particular pattern to receive ancestral protection.

Even today, many homes have "the good carpet" in the living room or guest space. We might not know why, but we still treat it with reverence.

During my childhood, rugs and carpets with traditional patterns were widely considered old-fashioned where I lived, suitable only for an old person's home. But even this negative connotation revealed some truth: Carpets are ancient, and they hold the very traditions that our grandparents still hold dear.

But actually, those "granny carpets" are coming back! Modern rugs may not always be handwoven or embroidered with intention, but the patterns endure. Fashion brought them back, of course, but the truth is they never really left. Geometric medallions, tree-of-life motifs, stylized flowers, hands, eyes, suns, and stars still appear in millions of homes across the world. Their origins are older than any nation, and their meanings—though mostly forgotten—still echo beneath our feet.

The Table and the Feast: Ancestral Echoes in the Dining Room

The dining room may seem like one of the most ordinary places in a modern home. But under the surface, it holds the memories of some of the oldest and most sacred rituals of human life. The act of sharing food, the arrangement of the table, the textile that covers it, the placement of plates and cups—none of these things are as casual as they seem. In many homes today, without even realizing it, we participate in ancient customs every time we set the table.

Let's begin with the heart of it all—the table.

For most ancient peoples, the table was sacred (and not at all the casual thing it is for us now). In early Indo-European and Semitic traditions, it was understood as a household altar: a place where offerings were put and the invisible could appear. The act of eating together around the table meant more than satisfying hunger. It was a ritual of declared peace, shared protection, and blessing. You were fed by the land, by the gods, and by the work of your ancestors. You made space for them, too, around the table. We should understand the amount of gratitude people once felt for having food in their homes. It wasn't wise to take it for granted. Food was cherished, and it wasn't guaranteed.

In some Slavic and Balkan traditions, a small piece of bread was left on the table overnight—not because someone might get hungry, but so that the house spirit or even an ancestor could share in the meal. The table was the place where the visible and invisible family members met. This is why, until very recently, many households in Eastern Europe would cover the table with a white cloth on the eve of a major holiday and leave food out for the dead overnight.

The place at the head of the table also has deep symbolic weight. It is the seat of honor—but it is also the axis around which order is maintained. The head of the table is where authority sits, where blessings are spoken, where the first toast or the first bite is taken. In ancient times, this seat was often reserved for an elder, the priest of the family, or the soul of the deceased family member. Even today in some traditions and families, it is considered inappropriate to sit there casually: It's a space that carries invisible weight.

And what about that curious superstition of not sitting at the corner of the table? This belief is still widespread in Slavic countries and in parts of Central and Southern Europe. "You won't get married if you do," they say. But beneath the joke lies something older and more serious. The corner, as a liminal point, was always associated with risk. Corners are thresholds. Spirits may gather there, especially uninvited ones. Sitting at a corner meant placing yourself at the edge—outside of the protective center of the table's blessing. It could signal exclusion, loneliness, or being "left out" of communal life. In many traditional homes, even today, children or guests are carefully guided to safer places around the table, away from the corners.

Now, let's look at what covers the table. Just like carpets, tablecloths were originally a form of protective magic. Slavic and Baltic embroidered linens often featured wide decorative borders, and, as you might have already guessed, those borders kept people safe. The threads acted like a fence, keeping the meal and its blessings "in," and warding off envious spirits or wandering forces. This logic is echoed in the patterns of woven towels (*rushnyky*) and even in the rim decorations on old ceramic plates and bowls. The logic is always the same: Wards around the edges keep danger away from the center.

The tablecloth itself was sometimes treated as a sacred item. In Romania and Ukraine, there was a belief that you could wrap sacred bread in the tablecloth during storms to protect the house. In some mountain regions, the holiday tablecloth would be used to bless livestock by shaking crumbs over their heads—so that the blessing of the feast would carry into the new season. In homes today, families keep special holiday linens, used only on Christmas, Easter, or for wedding celebrations.

Let's move to the dishes—the plates, the cups, the good silver. Many households still keep a glass cabinet or a special shelf for "the nice dishes." These are often pulled out only for holidays or important guests. But this habit is a modern version of an older magical custom. In many premodern societies, certain plates, pitchers, and utensils were used only for ritual meals: wedding feasts, harvest dinners, funeral wakes. They were stored carefully, passed down as heirlooms, and not used for everyday eating. Why? Because they had absorbed the memories of sacred events. They were "charged," in a way.

Some dishes were even believed to hold a kind of protective blessing after a ritual. In parts of Central Europe, it was common to drink from a shared cup during certain ceremonies and then store that cup safely in the family home, to become a kind of talisman. There are records from Germanic and Nordic folklore of cups kept from wedding feasts and used only again for funerals, or vice versa. These vessels marked the important moments of life and were not meant to be used casually.

And even today, we set the table with intention: We light candles, choose pretty napkins, open bottles of wine that have waited for just the right moment. In these intuitive acts, we rely upon our need to mark certain meals as different, as sacred. Whether it's a birthday dinner, a family reunion, or a simple Saturday night with friends—the impulse to make a feast, to honor it with special settings, is a way of stepping into ritual.

Even saying "bon appétit" or "bless this food" carries echoes of prayer. The table becomes a small altar again. We don't need to call it magic, but we still say the spell.

So next time you bring out the good dishes, smooth the tablecloth, or gently remind someone not to sit at the corner, you can smile a little. You're not being silly or sentimental. You're holding a thread that runs back through centuries—back to the sacred hearth, the ancestral table, and the feast that keeps the world turning.

The Bedroom: Veils, Shadows, and Spells of Rest

The bedroom is one of the most private spaces in the modern home—but that very privacy is a relatively recent invention. For most of human history, sleep was not a solitary activity. People slept communally, often all together in a single room, for warmth, safety, and necessity. The idea of a personal bedroom, let alone a "master bedroom," belongs to a much later stage of social and architectural development—and even then, it was a luxury, signaling both wealth and status.

Even when people shared sleeping space, they often found ways to mark off beds as special, sacred, and in need of magical protection. This was especially true for cradles and children's sleeping places. One of the most enduring traditions across cultures is the covering of the baby's bed—whether with a curtain, a veil, or a small canopy. Today we tend to think of these as charming or aesthetic additions, evoking softness, royalty, or vintage elegance. But their origins are far more serious: they were protective measures, meant to shield the most vulnerable members of the household from invisible forces.

In many European and Middle Eastern traditions, it was believed that infants could easily attract the attention of spirits—not all of them kind. A newborn's soul was still close to the other world, and that was both a blessing and a danger. Canopies and cradle curtains were convenient for blocking light or drafts: those purposes were important. But they were also spiritual shields—something that most parents would instinctively want for their newborn children. The fabric created a symbolic boundary, a soft veil between the baby and anything that might come wandering in during the night. Even in very modest homes, parents would do what they could to provide this protection.

The bed canopy itself follows the same magical logic. In cultures where adult beds had curtains or hangings, those too served as more than insulation. They created a sacred safe space within a room. Behind those curtains, dreams unfolded, bodies rested, lovers met, and, sometimes, lives ended. The bed was another threshold, though not as obvious as doors or windows. Sleep has always been understood as a vulnerable state: we leave our waking mind behind and drift into a world of spirits, dreams, ancestors' advice, and prophetic visions. The act of enclosing the bed with fabric mirrored older traditions of building symbolic protection around the sleeper.

Even the bed's orientation in the room was, and often still is, a matter of concern. In Slavic traditions, the bed should not be placed with the head near the door or in direct line with a mirror—both were considered dangerous. The mirror could trap or confuse the soul during sleep; the open door might let something in. In Chinese geomancy (feng shui), many similar rules apply: the bed should not face directly toward the door, the head should be against a solid wall, and clutter under the bed would interfere with spiritual flow. Also, if a local tradition advised burying the dead with a specific head orientation (head pointed to the west, feet headed east), then it was considered to be careless to orient the bed in that same way.

Rituals related to sleep persist quietly in modern habits, just like the other pieces of household magic. We shake out the sheets, we smooth the covers, we "air out" the bedroom—to tidy up, of course, but also from a deep instinct to renew the space and reset it. In many cultures, sleep is metaphorically linked to death and so are the morning rituals of waking, shaking off the night, and rejoining the world of the living.

Just like in ancient times, people still take special care of their sleeping spaces during major life events. In some cultures, the bed of a newly married couple is specially made by female relatives, blessed, or symbolically "opened" before the wedding night. In other places, beds are left empty and uncovered after a death, sometimes for several days. Even changing the sheets can feel like a small ritual. (Maybe stuffing a blanket into a duvet cover would be easier if we first made generous offerings to the spirits?)

The bedroom, with all its softness and quiet, holds the imprint of these old ideas. Early medieval European kings slept with lavender scattered all around the floor, making a primitive, but soft and scented, bed. And now one of the most popular bedroom aromas is lavender! Some things never really change, and even when they do, the deeper logic remains: The place where we sleep must be sacred, because we leave ourselves behind there. And something always waits to meet us, in the spaces where light gives way to shadow.

Soft Spells for the Little Ones

Children's rooms are often the most enchanted places in the house. Soft colors, tiny furniture, animals and stars painted on the walls, nightlights glowing like distant moons. It all feels a little bit like a fairy tale. And that's not by accident.

In many traditional cultures, young children were believed to be especially close to the spirit world. Not fully anchored yet, they were thought to still remember where they came from—and to be especially vulnerable to outside influences, both good and bad. For that reason, their spaces were carefully guarded. What now looks like charming decor stems from ancient protective magic.

For example, baby mobiles—those delicate things that hang above a crib—are among the oldest forms of home protection. Originally, they were made from herbs, feathers, bones, and sharp shapes like stars or arrows and were meant to scare away spirits and illnesses. In Slavic and Baltic traditions, mobiles were hung to spin slowly above babies, offering a moving shield of symbols. Even today, modern mobiles retain the same logic: they spin, they distract, and they bless the space.

Toys, too, began as protective objects. In many parts of the world, dolls were household guardians. In Eastern Europe, faceless rag dolls (*motanki*) were created without eyes or mouths so that no spirit could enter them. They were meant to absorb illness or misfortune and were sometimes ritually buried when they'd served their purpose. Wooden animals, often carved from household scraps, were totems of strength and fertility—especially horses, which were believed to carry good fortune. Pinwheels, tops, and spinning toys reflected the protective motion of the circle: a sacred, closed shape that repels harm.

Many of these toys are still around. The plush bear, whose ancestor was once a totemic forest guardian. The rocking horse, descended from sacred mounts of solar gods. And a spinning mobile above a sleeping baby keeps gently turning between worlds...

Daily Rituals of Cleansing and Care

A modern bathroom might seem like the least mystical place in the house—all practical and bright. But in truth, it holds one of the oldest rituals known to humankind: the sacred act of cleansing.

Across cultures and centuries, washing the body has always been a magical act, a spiritual reset, a way of restoring the soul's balance to the body. To cleanse oneself was to let go of unwanted energies, to break free from shadows, to return to one's center, and to make the body presentable for the gods. We still do it this way. A shower after a hard day lifts the weight of worries and crowds. A bath gathers scattered pieces of the self and dissolves stress. Many people speak of "feeling like themselves again" after bathing. That phrase is older than we think.

In ancient Rome, public baths were social but also deeply symbolic. Moving from hot to cold, pouring water, applying oils, resting in steam—all of it mimicked the stages of ritual purification. In many ritual scenarios, the act of entering sacred space required bathing first. In Shinto shrines in Japan, visitors still wash their hands and mouths before crossing the threshold. In Judaism and Islam, specific ablutions must be done before prayer. In Christianity, holy water blessed by priests is used to cleanse the ill and to dispel curses. The idea is always the same: Clean the body, and the spirit follows.

Bathing rituals were often accompanied by spoken prayers, herbs, oils, and symbols. Salt, now common in bath soaks, has long been one of the most powerful substances in magical traditions. It purifies, protects, and renews our connection with the earth. It was scattered across thresholds and stirred into water to banish harm. To this day, a warm bath with sea salt is one of the simplest and oldest magical cleansings a person can do, whether they know it or not.

Scented products echo the old herb baths and oil anointings of healers and priestesses. Lavender, rose, eucalyptus, mint—all these plants were once used in ritual washes, for both their physical and energetic properties. The modern shower gel or shampoo, promising "revival," "detox," or "glow," is just a polished descendant of ancient herbal potions. Marketing often leans into magical language: elixirs, potions, miracles in bottles. And rightly so. The bathroom shelf is a row of spell jars.

The process itself is fully ritualized. We undress—symbolic of shedding identity, roles, and burdens. We step under water—one of the powerful nature elements. We scrub, rub, and lather—gestures of exorcism, of renewal. Some people sing or hum—a sonic cleansing, an incantation. Some light candles, dim the lights, or close the door as if entering sacred space. We emerge damp and clean, like after baptism, rebirth, or healing. We wrap ourselves in towels like ritual garments and anoint our skin with creams and oils.

In many homes, the bath or shower is the only time of day when one is alone, naked, and unobserved—between the outer world and the inner one. It is, without being named so, a shrine of self-return.

There is even continuity with older communal bathing traditions. *Hammams* in the Islamic world, *banya* in Russia, sauna in the Nordic lands—all remain today not just as traditional practices or trendy spas, but as deeply cleansing rituals. Steam draws out what is hidden. Sweat is a sacrifice. Cold plunges shock the spirit awake. Birch twigs in a banya, aromatic oils in a sauna, clay masks in a hammam—all are ancient, healing gestures that still speak the language of folk magic.

A Power Spot in Every Home

Many people have a favorite place in their homes: a beloved armchair, a cozy corner for reading or breakfast, or even just a preferred chair at the table or a pillow on a wide windowsill. We rest in these places, we "recharge" there, and we often spend more time in them than is strictly necessary.

Coincidence or not, this habit also reaches deep into the magical past of the home. It was once believed that spirits lived in every corner. Over time, one could befriend the spirits that resided in a particular part of the house and even receive strength, energy, support, or protection from them.

In ancient Rome, this belief took on a very concrete form: People spoke of *genius loci*—the spirit of the place—and of minor deities that inhabited absolutely everything, from a doorpost to a cooking pot. The home was also shared with the spirits of the ancestors, known as *Lares* and *Penates*. The difference between them was mostly in scope:

The Lares were collective spirits of the household (including enslaved people), while the Penates were more personal—spirits inherited from one's family line. Both groups were worshipped and honored, and no proper home was considered complete without them.

Naturally, in a space so densely populated by invisible but powerful forces, people believed they could build special relationships with some representatives of these forces in particular. So the next time you settle into your favorite chair with a book, remember that quiet, friendly presence that—according to ancient tradition—might be the reason this corner of the home feels so special.

Evening Cleaning: How to Stay on Good Terms with the House

Leaving the home tidy and peaceful for the night simply feels good. Today, it's seen as a gesture of care toward the space, a way to preserve comfort, a natural ending to the day, and a small gift to your future self, who will wake up and start the day in a beautiful, calm environment.

But folklore gives this habit a deeper background: Leaving a mess overnight was believed anger the household spirits. In Slavic traditions, this custom is tied to two spirits in particular: the domovoy and the kikimora. Both seem to originate from ancient ancestor cults, but over time they evolved into very different beings in the folk imagination.

The domovoy is often pictured as a grandfatherly figure. He may pinch you, sit on your chest at night, or cause mischief if offended by neglect or disrespect—but overall, he's a helpful and protective spirit of the home. The kikimora, by contrast, is a more restless and malicious presence (likely a transformed image of a displeased ancestral spirit). If angered, she tangles thread, scratches under the floorboards, sours the milk, and pinches people in their sleep. But if no housework is left unfinished overnight, she can be appeased—and even becomes helpful. A woman with a satisfied kikimora in her home is said to get far more done than others.

Similar tales can be heard in other cultures as well—about brownies, *nisse*, *tomte*, and many other domestic spirits.

Traditionally, the evening cleaning would end with a small offering: a bowl of porridge or milk or a bit of bread left out for the household spirits. Few people still follow this custom today, though it still lives on quietly in some homes. But the spirits don't seem offended. For those who leave the house clean and orderly at night, the spirits offer a lighter morning and a comforting sense of balance.

Small Spells for Your Home

- Sweep the front doorstep with nine firm strokes. You are clearing a path for many blessings.

- Rub a small bit of salt into the doormat. It turns away what has no kindness.

- Place a coin on the windowsill. Say, "Guardians of thresholds, keep watch." It's a deal now.

- Arrange your three favorite mugs in a triangle on the shelf. This is now a charm of morning peace.

- Kiss your hand and press it against the bedroom wall before sleeping. Let it be a silent promise of safety.

- Tie a bit of green thread around a chair leg. It keeps the spirit of the home anchored during hard days.

- Sit on the rug with bare feet and press your palms to it. Say nothing. Let the house feel your presence inside this magical field.

- Offer the fireplace (or a candle) a piece of bark, a paper with a joyful scribble or your favorite lyrics, or a poem you wrote. Homes love small offerings.

- After you've tidied up, make a cup of tea, hold it with both hands, and say aloud: "This house and I care for each other." Sip slowly, knowing that the walls will agree.

Chapter 6

Magical Food

Spells you can eat—why food has always been part of rituals, celebrations, and healing.

There has never been such a thing as an ordinary meal. To eat is to commune with your own body, with your family or friends, and with earth, fire, history, and spirits. In every culture, the act of making and sharing food has always been more than practical. It is magic at its most intimate: a ritual we perform daily, often without realizing how old and sacred the gestures truly are.

Long before temples, there were hearths. Scholars like Richard Wrangham have argued that the mastery of fire—and the invention of cooking—was not just a technological leap, but the very spark of civilization itself. The earliest communities formed around hearths. Recipes, though unwritten, were passed down like spells, bread was broken in reverence, salt was offered to spirits, honey sealed oaths and healed wounds. To cook was to transform, and to eat was to receive that transformation into your body.

Across time and space, food has served as an offering, a medicine, a sign from the gods, and a token of supernatural entities' goodwill. In ancient Greece, libations of wine and oil were poured for the dead. In Japan, rice is still left on family altars. In Slavic and Greek traditions, a special sweet dish made of cottage cheese was strongly connected with the world of the dead and with resurrection. Every ingredient carried meaning: eggs held the sun, milk meant life, garlic equaled protection, apples contained joy and desire... And grain was seen and treated as the body of the earth herself.

In this chapter, we won't cover every food's enchantment; though in truth, all food is—and has always been—sacred. Instead, we'll turn our focus to a handful of ingredients that echo across cultures and epochs—each one thick with symbolism and centuries of magical history.

These are the foods that once fed gods and ghosts. The ones that carry wishes, protect love, and whisper old secrets right from your plate. Their magic is already in your kitchen. Let's begin.

Small Spell for Charmed Boiling

When a pot comes to boil, wave your hand gently over the steam and murmur something you never say aloud. Let the kitchen eat the secret and keep it warm for you.

Magic Baked into a Loaf: Why Bread Is Sacred

There is a Russian saying: "bread is everything's head," meaning that bread is the most important food for every meal. Such reverence for bread was widespread across agricultural cultures—countless rituals and customs are associated with it. A full book wouldn't be enough to cover them all, so let's take a look at a few vivid examples and draw some parallels to how we perceive bread today.

In ancient Greece, bread was offered to many gods—but especially to those who participated in its creation, the goddesses of grain and agriculture (Ceres, Demeter). Bread was associated with fullness and was essentially a synonym for food—the primary product of the earth, the foundation of life. Interestingly, even today bread is often unconsciously perceived as the default food—despite the fact that most of us don't rely on it as a staple. In certain idioms and common phrases, "bread" stands for food or—even more broadly—for livelihood or sustenance. For example: "make some dough" or being the "breadwinner," and so on.

In ancient Rome, *libum* were a kind of round honey cheesecake. They had magical and religious functions and were also offered to household spirits.

In medieval Europe, there were many fascinating folk magic rituals involving bread. For example, blessed bread was kept as a charm against illness, curses, or lightning. There were customs of preserving Christmas bread (for instance, in France, *pain de Noël*) as protection for the coming year.

Perhaps one of the most striking bread-related rituals was the funerary flatbread made with the ashes of ancestors by some Native American peoples, such as the Navajo and Hopi. Bread was linked with the dead—but it was also a symbol of life and body. Such duality is typical for the most sacred objects or symbols.

Bread is unique in that it carries the symbolism of both "default food" (food in its purest form) and "not just food" (something magical, powerful, and easily infused with sacred meanings). This is still reflected in many households through taboos resembling ritual prohibitions—you mustn't drop it, cut it the wrong way, or leave it unfinished (some people still refuse to throw away breadcrumbs, instead feeding them to birds).

There are also many modern rituals where bread plays the central role: Easter *kulich* or cake, the wedding *karavay* in Slavic traditions, Christian communion, and many others. Bread or home baking still symbolizes comfort, harmony, and the warmth of a good home. It may not be obvious, but think of how books or films depict a cozy house with a loving family—you almost always find a pie baking in the oven.

The most magical product of ancient times has remained our "basic," essential, everyday product. Coincidence? More likely, cultural continuity.

Round Like the Sun

Bread loaves were often made in the shape of a circle, and this was especially important when the bread was made for ritual purposes: It represents the sun and the cycle of life and rebirth with it.

But in fact, all round foods shared this symbolism, like pies (for example, those blueberry ones made by Celts for Lughnasadh), pancakes (Eastern Slavic *bliny* for *Maslennitsa*, the spring equinox celebration), cookies (in medieval Europe, they were called soul cakes and given to beggars on All Souls Day Eve so they could pray for deceased relatives), and even cheeses (rolled from the hills in ritual contests across old Europe). Round food was sacred food, and we still love it, even if we don't think of it as a little sun in our kitchen anymore.

> *Small Spell: Pie Spell for Protection*
>
> When making or serving pie, press your thumb gently into the crust or fruit and say, "Stay sweet, stay safe." The spell works best with shared slices.

The Meaning and Magic of Milk

Milk is another ancient substance rich in sacred connotations. Its symbolism was different from that of bread. Milk was white and fed newborn beings and was therefore closely tied to the idea of purity. It was the first fresh food after a long winter—in many cultures, it marked the beginning of renewal and the return of life. This is reflected, for example, in the Celtic festival of Imbolc, held in early February. The name is most often interpreted as "in milk" or "in the womb."

Purity as the main quality of milk is also harnessed by folk divination. Milk was used to detect curses or magical harm supposedly caused by witches or spirits: If the milk curdled or lost its smooth appearance after certain actions, it meant something was wrong—impure. If it stayed fresh and uniform, then the person or object in question was considered clean as well.

Another symbolic meaning of milk—and a very natural one—is care, maternal nourishment, comfort, and safety. Milk sustains life from birth and continued to provide nourishment even during times when meat was ritually forbidden (for example, during fasting periods).

A glass of warm milk at night is still more than just a drink—it's something symbolic, like a gentle potion we've known since childhood. Those who don't drink cow's milk often treat plant-based alternatives the same way. We believe milk can calm us, ease our worries, help us relax and fall asleep. That belief is the same one our distant ancestors had.

Small Spell: The Milk of Kindness

Pour a splash of milk into your tea or pot and stir clockwise. Think of someone who cared for you as a child. That warmth stays in the drink, like a charm for softness and inner ease.

"Honey" Has Always Meant "Dear"...

Food of light, of the soul, and of the spirit world. Food of the gods… and their gift. A symbol of pleasure and a blessed, joyful life. All of this describes honey, another sacred substance, stirred into magic just as often as we stir it into tea or warm milk.

Honey, in essence, embodies everything good—everything people desire and long for. It was used for healing, spread on doorways to ward off evil spirits, given as a blessing... One magical ingredient that was useful in just about any situation? Honey.

Another symbolic side to honey is binding, connecting, glueing, or sealing a bond. In Russian, there's still an expression that literally translates as "Was it spread with honey there?"—meaning "Why are you so drawn to this?" That's why it was used both as a medium for contacting the dead and as a popular ingredient in love magic. Offering someone a drink sweetened with honey was a way to bind them to you, to create and strengthen emotional ties. In fact, the modern word *honeymoon* comes from the tradition of giving newlyweds honey wine for a lunar month after the wedding to enhance love and encourage conception.

The golden light of the sun, the strength and scent of flowers, the labor of bees and beekeepers—these all combine to give honey an aura of absolute worth, as a kind of wonder-elixir. When we stir a spoonful of honey into tea for someone who's sick or into milk for a child at bedtime, we're repeating a small ritual that once held huge meaning.

Small Spell: Honey Blessing for the Tongue

Dip your finger in honey and touch it to your lips before a hard conversation. Say nothing until the sweetness sinks in. Words become gentler when blessed.

The Eternal Egg

What if our world came from an egg? Physicists might not agree—but that's exactly what the ancient Greeks believed. In the Orphic myths, our universe was born from the Cosmic Egg. An egg has a clear structure: an outer shell, an inner nourishing layer of white, and a hidden golden core. In a way, it's a perfect model for any system—whether it's the human body (bones and internal organs wrapped in tissue, all encased in protective layers of skin) or the cosmos itself (the sky surrounding the earth, which hides the underworld below).

As this kind of "miniature universe," eggs became indispensable in folk magic: They were used to absorb negativity from sick people. To this day, at least in Slavic countries, people still remove curses by "rolling out" the body with an egg and use eggs to cleanse the energy of a space where something unsettling has happened.

Another magical meaning of the egg is rebirth—that endless "chicken or egg" cycle where no beginning or end can be found. The eternal rhythm of birth, death, and birth again—this is exactly what the egg so clearly and beautifully represents. In some Balkan villages, people still place an egg in the coffin of the deceased. This custom is ancient—there's even a theory that it was practiced by the Celts who lived in the Balkans before the Slavic tribes arrived. Christian priests have tried hard to eliminate this ritual, but it refuses to die out—it keeps resurfacing and returning to folk tradition.

Rebirth and eggs are closely linked across many cultures—especially when we think of the role eggs play in modern Easter celebrations. Where I live, you can't escape eggs during the Easter season—they're everywhere: stickers and dye kits in every supermarket, rabbit and chick figurines with eggs, egg-hunt kits in home stores, and cafe windows filled with garlands of colorful eggs.

Even if you don't celebrate Easter yourself, you're surrounded by these symbols. Now we know why: They remind us that spring is the season of nature's return. And maybe—just maybe—they're also here to suggest that the human soul might be eternal too, destined to be reborn again and again, triumphing over death.

> *Small Spell: Egg Ritual of Beginnings*
> Hold an egg in your hands before cracking it. Think of something new you'd like to hatch into your life. Let the yolk carry that wish into the next world.

An Apple a Day Keeps the Magic Around

The apple is one of the most symbolically rich and magically charged fruits. It has played a role in all kinds of magic—from blessings to curses. But its dominant magical meaning is love.

In ancient Greece, it was the fruit of the love goddess Aphrodite. In ancient Rome, giving someone an apple was a way of declaring love. In Slavic love divination, a girl would eat an apple before bed and say, "The one who's destined for me, come to me in a dream." In the love magic of medieval Europe, there was a simple but widely believed ritual: lovers who ate an apple together would stay together forever.

In the Balkans, apples are still used in wedding ceremonies: Coins are pressed into the fruit, and it's given to the bride as a talisman. The gesture is meant to bless the marriage with both love and riches. In ancient graves, archaeologists have found the same kinds of coin-filled apples placed with young women and girls—those who died before marrying. Before burial, they were given symbolic "posthumous weddings," repeating the rituals of a real one.

The apple also carries another meaning—that of an enchanted fruit that grows between worlds. In Ireland and Wales, apples belonged to the Tuatha Dé Danann, the magical people of the goddess Danu who lived on the land before humans arrived. In British and Scottish folklore, apples were linked to autumn and death—but not as an ending, rather as a transition to a new cycle. This in-between quality gave apples special status: They crossed seasonal and symbolic boundaries, remaining edible in summer, autumn, and winter, and were believed to hold otherworldly magic.

Interestingly, the apple tree wasn't forgotten even in winter. Among the Celts—and later in medieval England—there were traditions of "wassailing" the apple trees on the night of the winter solstice: pouring cider or ale at their roots, dancing around them, thanking them for last year's harvest, and waking them to bear fruit again.

Today, apples seem like a simple fruit—even a "default fruit"; for many, it's the first one that comes to mind. But that simplicity is deceiving. Across cultures, we find echoes of the apple's deeper magic and power, from the golden Apple of Discord that sparked the Trojan War and the biblical "forbidden fruit" (which only became an apple in medieval Europe) to the poisoned apple that sent Snow White into her long sleep (and, in a strange way, also brought her love and a happy ending).

Garlic (Not Just Against Vampires)

Everywhere garlic was used, it was associated with powerful protection. Today, thanks to pop culture, we know that garlic keeps vampires away—but its protective power is far older than any vampire legend.

In ancient Greece, garlic was considered a plant of the dead; in some regions, garlic is still used in funeral and remembrance rituals. It was offered to spirits and to gods of the underworld. At the same time, there was always a strong belief that garlic gave strength and warded off evil; for example, Roman soldiers ate garlic before going into battle.

In medieval Europe, garlic was primarily used to guard against disease: It was placed by the bedsides of the sick, hung in barns, and added to herbal remedies. Garlic clearly shows the deep overlap between folk magic and folk medicine—a pattern seen with many other herbs and vegetables too. It was used (and still is) to protect the home from any kind of harm and to protect the body from disease. Long before this was confirmed by science, people somehow recognized garlic's protective qualities. It really does activate the immune system and contains allicin, a compound with antibacterial, antiviral, and antifungal properties.

These very real protective qualities were extended to more subtle realms, and garlic came to be used against both illness and spirits. Among the Slavic peoples, windowsills, doorframes, and thresholds were thoroughly rubbed with garlic to protect the household from anything harmful, from witches and restless spirits to the evil eye and illness. Similar practices are found in the American South as well.

Who knows? Maybe those cloves of garlic in your cabinet are quietly guarding you from dark energies.

Small Spell: Garlic Ward at the Threshold

Hang a clove of garlic near the door or tuck one into your pantry. Every kitchen is a hearth, and every hearth deserves its own teeth against trouble.

Salt: Too Precious to Be Ordinary

Do you know the origin of the word *salary*? No one knows for certain, but there is a fascinating theory. In ancient Rome, salt was so valuable that some soldiers were allegedly paid in salt for their service—that payment was called *salarium*.

In Greece, salt was honored as a pure and sacred substance. Homer called it "divine." It was used in purification rituals and was always present at sacred feasts as an essential element of hospitality and connection with the gods. Food prepared with salt was considered worthy of the gods; food without it was for humans only and was suitable for ordinary days, but never for holidays or anything sacred. Salt was seen as a pure element that repelled evil through its very cleanliness. It was placed in houses' foundation during construction, sprinkled on the walls and left in the rooms' corners, and even rubbed onto newborn babies—all for protection.

In the Middle Ages, salt came to symbolize value and unbreakable deals. To share salt with someone, especially at the table, meant to form a sacred bond. Because of this sacred status (and possibly its high cost), spilling salt was seen across Europe as an omen of conflict or misfortune. To counter it, people would throw a pinch of the spilled salt over their left shoulder—straight into the devil's face.

In Afro-Caribbean and hoodoo traditions, salt is a key tool in cleansing and protective magic. It's scattered across thresholds, sprinkled on the footprints of enemies, and used to create magical circles of protection—just like in modern mainstream witchcraft, where salt circles are considered a basic way to mark ritual space and keep harmful forces out.

In contemporary Russian witchcraft, a special kind of salt is especially beloved: black Thursday salt. It's made on Holy Thursday during Passion Week—an Orthodox tradition—but its magical use goes far beyond Christianity. This salt is used as protection while traveling and more broadly as a charm against misfortune. Like ordinary salt, it's sometimes sprinkled in the corners of the house.

It's amazing how this ancient practice survived through centuries of history—including seventy years of Soviet atheism and the fight against superstition.

Today, we rarely think of salt as something special, but, in reality, we're dealing with one of the most precious substances of the ancient world—and one of the most magical. That connection has been preserved more clearly in magic than in cooking: The salt circles used in ritual work or bath salts mixed with other powerful ingredients are now part of many people's spiritual or recreational practice around the world.

But it's important to remember that, in the old days, salt was considered magical all by itself—in any food or on the table—not only as part of some elaborate spell.

Small Spell: Draw a Circle of Safety with Salt

Before you begin cooking something important, trace a small circle of salt on the counter, just big enough for your favorite utensil to rest inside. That's your kitchen guardian now.

The Ancient Potion

Wine has always been seen as a magical drink—after all, it literally changes the state of the person who drinks it, transforming perception, mood, and, it seems, the very reality around them.

These shifts were felt as a movement toward the divine—or at the very least a way to share a drink fit for the gods themselves.

Grapes, accordingly, were considered sacred—and were often entrusted to powerful and influential deities. In ancient Greece, for instance, grapevines belonged to Dionysus (known as Bacchus in Rome)—the god of fertility, transformation, ecstasy, and madness. Among the Slavs, grapes were sacred to Veles—the god of the underground world (including the realm of the dead), magic, livestock, poetry, and many other vital aspects of human life.

In many cultures, wine was poured as an offering—to the roots of trees, onto the ground, over graves... This tradition survives to this day: In Eastern Europe, pouring wine on a grave is a common gesture of memory and reverence. Stronger alcohol is sometimes used the same way. It's also considered a potent substance for spirit contact, and people believe that, in the afterlife, the soul can drink through the offering.

But while hard liquor was seen as a powerful gift for spirits, wine carried an additional meaning—it was life-giving, beneficial. It was believed to nourish not only spiritual entities but the earth itself—and, as I've mentioned earlier, it was even suitable for the gods.

In medieval Europe, breaking a bottle of wine together after sealing a deal was a way to invite God—or magical beings and spirits—to act as a witness and to bless the venture with the life-giving power of wine.

Wine was also an essential part of festivals, rituals, weddings, and funerary meals. It was used not only as food but as medicine:

wine infused with herbs, garlic, cinnamon, or rosemary. These mixtures were often seen as magical in nature—the power of the wine combined with the powers of each added ingredient, creating something stronger. People truly believed these remedies would work, and often recited spells, formulas, or prayers as they drank them.

Wine was present at every festive table throughout the year, but sometimes it was given its own special day. Each folk tradition had its own version. Interestingly, in Serbia and Bulgaria, grapevines are still honored on Saint Tryphon's Day—February 14. On this day, vines are trimmed, sprinkled with wine, and prayed over for a good harvest—as if we are showing the vine what its final product will be, born from its labor together with humans.

February 14 as a wine and grape festival may be just coincidence, but wine does have a leading role in love magic. Wine mixed with honey—and sometimes with less pleasant ingredients—was given to a beloved. Like in the legend of Tristan and Isolde, this kind of potion was believed to create mutual, powerful, and eternal love. These rituals existed all over Europe—and perhaps beyond, too. Even today, if you search online for a love spell, you're very likely to find one or more recipes involving wine.

The power of the grape—and the drink it gives us—lies in the way it leads us to the threshold (and thresholds are precisely where magic is believed to happen). It's the boundary between wakefulness and sleep which intoxication brings us to, more or less. It's the boundary between the living and the dead—both of whom, it seems, will gladly share a glass of wine. It's also the boundary between gods and mortals—since wine is deeply linked to the divine world and may even come from it.

And today, wine is also a link between the ancient and the modern—it's fair to say that wine still tastes like old magic.

> *Small Spell: Wine-Whispering Spell*
>
> Before pouring wine, tap the neck of the bottle with your fingernail three times. The first tap is for laughter, the second for courage, the third for grace.

Beer for Gods, Witches, Farmers, and Earth Spirits

Beer is one of the oldest alcoholic beverages in the world. As long as six thousand years ago, it was brewed in Mesopotamia and Egypt. It was made from barley, wheat, and millet—the same grains that were at the heart of agrarian life.

In Sumerian tradition, brewing was overseen by the goddess Ninkasi, and there was even a hymn to Ninkasi that served as both a recipe and a ritual text.

In Ancient Egypt, beer was the drink of the dead: It was placed in tombs along with bread so that the soul wouldn't go hungry. It was also included in offerings to gods and ancestral spirits.

In Scandinavia, beer was the drink of Asgard. In the *Poetic Edda*, there are mentions of gods drinking beer, of magical honey being brewed (a drink between mead and beer), and of beer being a gift and a weapon—something with the power to influence fate.

In medieval Europe, beer was brewed both by monks (in monasteries, as part of the "spiritual diet") and by witches (at least according to popular lore). Witches were often shown with a cauldron—not only because they were thought to brew potions, but also because brewing beer was seen as a craft closely tied to magic given its components: water, fire, grain, yeast, and time.

In fact, even the iconic witch's hat may have started as the hat worn by female brewers. In the Middle Ages and especially the early modern period (fourteenth to seventeenth centuries), women often brewed beer at home in small batches and sold it at local markets. This was a perfectly ordinary occupation—especially in England, Germany, and Scandinavia. These women were known as alewives or brewsters. They had a recognizable outfit: a tall, pointed hat so they could be seen in a crowd and a long apron.

Often, a broom was placed by the door to show that beer was available. Sometimes, there was also a cauldron or a vat of malt and hops visible nearby. In other words, the classic witch image—hat, cauldron, broom—was actually that of a beer-seller.

The problem was that brewing became more and more profitable. And over time, male guilds and town authorities began to push women out of the trade. To do this, they used a common strategy of the era: accusing women of witchcraft. Female brewers were demonized through rumors that they enchanted their customers, spoke with spirits, or added potions to their beer... These stories were used to bar them from selling, seize their property, and even persecute them as witches. And so this "witch look" became a caricature—a way to discredit and drive women out of a profitable craft.

This is part of a much broader historical pattern: the link between accusations of witchcraft and economic pressure on women, especially those with independent incomes, herbal knowledge, and local ritual expertise. In this sense, the witch's hat wasn't initially a symbol of sorcery—it was a symbol of independence, skill, knowledge, and labor that was turned into an accusation.

In Russia and the Balkans, beer or fermented grain drinks were sometimes poured into the earth as offerings—especially on Trinity Sunday or days of remembrance for the dead, like Parents' Saturday. Like wine, beer was used in funerary rites, especially in Northern and Eastern Europe. People poured it on graves or brought it into the home on memorial days. It is still practiced. Walking around cemeteries in Serbia, I frequently notice beer cans left on the graves for the dead. It seems that the love of beer is something that can't be lost even when you die. The living and the dead are united in their desire for the foamy drink.

And indeed, in folklore, beer was considered a "people's drink," a symbol of joy, fertility, shared labor, and celebration after work. In American and British rural traditions, beer was drunk at harvest festivals like Harvest Home, and special seasonal brews were made—autumn ale, wedding ale, Christmas ale. Recipes often included spices, honey, herbs, and even spoken charms—traditional verbal formulas to bless the brew, passed down by families.

If wine carried the aura of "high magic," beer in folk tradition had more everyday, earthy magic. It was fit for literally everyone, from gods and dead relatives to friends and family.

If household objects and daily meals still don't seem magical to you, don't be discouraged. We're entering an even more arcane zone now: archaic protection charms and initiation rituals. If you are prepared to find an unexpected ritual or two in your own life, read on!

Chapter 7

Protection Spells (Even Those We're Barely Noticing)

*Warding off evil with everything from salt lines
to lullabies and lucky charms.*

Protection is one of the primary functions of magic. Safety is such a basic necessity that we humans have invented countless ways, both practical and spiritual, to stay as safe as possible. It is obvious that we wish to keep not only ourselves safe, but everything and everyone we love and cherish: family, home, health, future… There is also a simpler kind of magical protection; with daily spells, we try to keep our food, our sleep, our travel, and our deals safe. Yes, we still do that! Protection magic is the one that has proved itself to be most resilient to time, science, and technology. Protection magic is still built into our lives, from habits at home to rules of polite behavior. The next time someone says, "Bless you!" when you sneeze, remember that strong spiritual meaning lies in the core of this automatic response designed to guard you from misfortune and evil.

Looking at your daily life from this perspective, you can see how well-protected we still are—even if we don't all believe in the forces we're keeping ourselves safe from.

Little Spells for Liminal Moments

When someone sneezes, we say "Bless you," almost without thinking. But this tiny habit has ancient roots. Ancient Greeks believed that a sneeze could be a divine sign. This is still alive in the Russian belief that a sneeze is a magical confirmation that the phrase said right before it was 100 percent true. But in medieval Europe, sneezing became a moment of danger. A sneeze could mean illness, a risk of demonic possession, or death. Saying "Bless you" was a way of offering swift protection and invoking divine mercy. Today, in many languages, the reflex remains: From the German *"Gesundheit"* to the Russian *"bud' zdorov,"* people still bless each other's health after every sneeze. The spell is in the saying: fast, sincere, and directed at the sneezer's breath (or soul's doorway).

There are many other small moments that require protection. If you speak of something good—your health, your luck, your child's cleverness—there's a risk you might attract the eye of something envious. That's why we knock on wood. In some versions of this ritual, the wood is sacred: a tree inhabited by a spirit or the wood of the cross. In others, the gesture is a way to interrupt what you've just said, to break the sentence before fate hears it and decides to punish your pride. Knock twice, sometimes three times, and the danger is scattered: a quiet, tactile counterspell.

The same fear of tempting fate is behind spitting over the left shoulder. In Slavic, Balkan, Greek, and Jewish traditions, saliva is a powerful magical ingredient, and spitting over the left shoulder sends it toward the realm of spirits—because the left side was long believed to be the side of demons and the dead. Saying *tfu-tfu-tfu* mimics the sound of spitting, but it works just as well. It's a hissing ward, a way to scatter any listening spirits who might twist your good fortune into harm. It can follow a compliment, a worry, or even a dream.

Spilling salt is another accident that calls for a quick magic solution. Salt is an ancient protector—costly, incorruptible, and often used in rituals to keep spirits at bay. To waste it was unlucky, and to leave it spilled was worse. But if you acted fast and threw a pinch over your left shoulder, you sent that protective force back into the realm it came from. Some say the salt hits the devil in the eye; others say it blinds fate before it has time to notice your mistake. Either way, it's a moment when instinct becomes ritual.

And then there's "jinx"—a modern word with old, tangled roots. If two people speak the same word or phrase at the same time, it creates a ripple in the air, a little shock in the rhythm of the world. In English-speaking countries, children say "jinx!" to claim temporary power: The other can't speak again until their name is said or a ritual is performed. The word itself may come from *iynx*, a kind of magical bird in Greek lore which is invoked in love spells and bindings. There's something uncanny about unison speech, something that hints at synchronicity, luck, or even danger; a broken pattern. In folk logic, if your words align with someone else's, it might mean you're not entirely alone: Something invisible might be echoing through you both. So we jinx, we laugh, and we break the moment before it can stretch into something spooky.

Verbal Formulas for Protection

Magical protection often takes the shape of lullabies. Their melodies soothe and help a child fall asleep, but it's the words that build the magic. Almost every culture has lullabies that cast a veil between the baby and harm.

In old Slavic lullabies, wolves, winds, and thieves appear again and again. They are spoken aloud and named, so they may be appeased or kept away. "Sleep, my baby, or the gray wolf will come," sounds frightening only on the surface. In truth, it's a kind of protective bargain—if the danger is acknowledged, it might not need to come. Often, a blessing follows right after: "Spit on evil, let the dream be kind." The rhythm, the repetition, and the naming—all of it follows a common structure of a protective incantation.

In Gaelic traditions, Scottish and Irish lullabies like "Baloo Baleerie" or "Seoithín Seó" invoke saints, ancestors, or the spirits of the hearth itself to protect the sleeping child. These songs invoke the hidden world to stand guard—something between a prayer and a spell.

In Turkish lullabies, phrases like "düşmesin aklına kötü düşler" ("may bad dreams not come into your mind") are spoken with the cadence of prayer. They are wishes shaped into rhythm. In Japanese lullabies, like the Edo Lullaby, the absent mother is replaced by a guardian figure—a promise that someone is watching. In West African lullabies, spirits and ancestors are sometimes asked to cradle the baby's soul while the body sleeps.

* * *

Beyond lullabies, spoken charms for protection are hidden in daily language all around the world.

In Italy, some people say "Gesù, Maria, e Giuseppe" when a child seems unwell or startled—an invocation to shield them from fright. Irish expressions like "God between us and all harm" are still spoken during travel or uncertainty. In England and Appalachia, older folk might still say "Speak of the devil and he appears"—it's an idiom about the appearance of someone just mentioned, but it describes the ancient belief that some things are best not spoken aloud if you don't want to meet them in person.

In the Middle East and North Africa, "*Mashallah*" is spoken when admiring a child, a plant, or a new home—deflecting envy before it can settle. In Arabic, "*Bismillah*" ("in the name of God") is said before opening a door, serving food, or even beginning a journey. These are very ancient charms in a sacred form.

* * *

Whispered blessings, muttered warnings, nonsense rhymes meant to keep a child from tripping—these are all ways of calling for safety, of creating it out of thin air. Language gives shape to fear, and by allowing us to shape it, it gives us power. The spells don't have to sound old and spooky. Sometimes, they're just phrases we've heard a thousand times—words passed down through so many generations that their magic became invisible, mundane…but still dear to us.

The Power of the Obscene

Not all protection spells are nice. Since ancient times, there has been a belief that foul language and obscene gestures can scare off evil—especially the kind that thrives on politeness and fear. When facing misfortune, sometimes it helps to get a little rude.

Swearing has deep magical roots. In ancient Rome, oaths and curses were close siblings: *Iuro* ("I swear") and *iuro per deos infernos* ("I swear by the gods below") were formulas meant not just to promise, but to bind reality. Early Germanic and Slavic tribes used strong, taboo-breaking language in protective rituals: The idea was that a sudden, jarring obscenity could disrupt evil's approach, like a shout that breaks one's concentration.

Even now, it is common to respond to bad news with a muttered curse—not necessarily aimed at anyone but rather cast out like a warding flare. The more vulgar the phrase, the stronger the shield. People instinctively blurt out rude words when startled or threatened, forgetting that initially they were used for protection—but still calling to that power.

And then there are the gestures. The fig sign—a thumb stuck between the joining of two fingers—can still be seen on amulets in Italy, Brazil, and the Balkans. From a modern perspective, it looks childish, even ridiculous. But this symbol, which mimics male sexual anatomy and is used as a rude gesture of refusal, was once a weapon against the evil eye. In Roman times, it was carved into household charms, worn on jewelry, and given to children to keep them safe. And, of course, it was used in the presence of anything (or anyone) unwanted.

The middle finger carries a similar past. Long before it became a sign of insult, it was used in ancient Greece as a crude phallic symbol to ward off misfortune. The logic was the same: shock the spirits, mock the demons, and make them turn away in disgust or confusion. The obscene was a kind of spiritual camouflage: If you looked wild or repulsive enough, nothing would want to take you. It was also a way to demonstrate, as if telling otherworldly forces: "We humans have a power of our own!"

In many traditional societies, ugliness and vulgarity were protective. That's why grotesque masks are worn during festivals and why noisy, lewd songs were sung during liminal moments like weddings and funerals. Many cultures still believe that children must be mocked or insulted a little when they look too cute or healthy, lest the spirits grow jealous. That's where phrases like "What an ugly baby" or "Get out of here, rascal" come from, said with a smile and a protective hand.

To be obscene, then, is not always bad. In older systems of thought, it was sometimes the only way to be safe. We still carry these habits today, half as jokes, half as instinct: a sharp curse when you drop something, a rude sign to ward off someone's ill will, a little traditional mockery to keep the spirits disoriented. Who said that magic always has to be reverent and polite? When it comes to defending oneself, it's often better to show the evil forces some teeth (or a certain finger).

Daily Spells Against All Evil

Some protective rituals have never quite disappeared. They've been practiced for centuries, passed along quietly by tradition or rumor. Even if someone says they don't believe in "that sort of thing," there's a good chance they perform some of these spells exactly as their grandmother did. Because when it comes to protection, we all tend to stick with what seems to work—even if we're not sure how.

Scattering salt across the threshold after cleaning is one of the most enduring household protections. It's usually the last act, after sweeping and mopping. A thin line of salt is placed along the door, or a few pinches are added to the corners. Sometimes it's followed by a blessing, sometimes not. Salt was always a ward, and the threshold, as a liminal space, needs watching. A salt line keeps whatever's bad out and marks the cleaning as complete both physically and spiritually.

Pouring wine around the perimeter of a house or yard is still done quietly in many places, especially before major gatherings or after gossip has disturbed the atmosphere. A discreet pour near each corner—sometimes paired with a whispered wish or cross-shaped motion—wards off envy and ill will. Wine is celebratory, but also sacrificial; when spilled for protection, it does its work exactly the way it did thousands of years ago. It is quite interesting that this method of simple protection has become popular on social media lately, with many people sharing videos of them pouring wine (or grape juice) around their yards. Many of those people claim that it isn't witchcraft, "This just works, that's all."

Holy water is another protective substance easily found in many homes. It is often used against all kinds of paranormal activity. When people are scared of ghosts or other eerie creatures, they sprinkle the holy water around themselves and their homes. Those people might not be religious or superstitious most of the time, but if something uncanny spooks them, they, quite logically, think that the solution should be just as "magical" as the problem.

Amulets of Safety

Many amulets worn today as jewelry or accessories were originally protective charms. Their symbolism and function evolved over centuries, but traces of their magical origins remain surprisingly persistent.

Perhaps the most obvious example, the red string tied around the wrist, is used across many cultures (from the Balkans to the Kabbalistic tradition) as a protective barrier against the evil eye. Its color alone has ancient associations with life force, blood, and power; red is believed to confuse or repel harmful spirits and hostile intentions. In some Slavic regions, red thread is tied not only to people, but also on infants' cribs, animal horns, or doorknobs. The gesture protects by drawing attention and absorbing harm.

The evil eye amulet, often shaped like a blue eye, is one of the most widespread magical symbols in the world. It serves both as a representation of the gaze and as its counterforce: a watching eye that repels other, malevolent eyes. These amulets are worn in Greece, Turkey, parts of the Middle East and Latin America, and increasingly as aesthetic jewelry, though their function is still understood intuitively. The shape may vary, but the purpose remains: to break the dangerous force of envy.

Wearing a cross is often associated with religious identity, but originally it was a protective sign. The form of the cross predates Christianity; it appeared in Bronze Age cultures carved into household objects or worn on the body. Whether in the form of two sticks tied together, etched on doors, or worn around the neck, the crossing lines have long marked boundaries and invoked balance and justice.

The safety pin, once used to fasten clothing and baby swaddles, became a common amulet against the evil eye in Eastern Europe. Pinned inside a child's clothes—especially turned downward or hidden from view—it was believed to "catch" malicious attention before it could reach the child. The gesture of pinning something closed to keep evil out dates back to iron-age traditions, where sharp metal objects were thought to repel spirits and malicious sorcery.

Wearing clothes inside out is still a folk remedy for sudden fear, disorientation, or "bad luck," and serves as a way to confuse or repel evil spirits. This belief was particularly strong in Slavic, Baltic, and Finno-Ugric traditions, where spirits were said to follow the known outline of a person. Turning garments inside out made the wearer temporarily unrecognizable to harmful forces and left the spirits confused and preoccupied with solving this shapeshifting mystery.

Even the most ordinary items of clothing once had built-in protective meaning. Belts, for instance, symbolized personal power and integrity. To "gird oneself" was to mark a boundary between the inner and outer self. Necklaces and bracelets began as boundary markers around the throat and wrists, vulnerable body parts. Braids and hair ornaments could bind and protect the head and spirit.

In Slavic cultures, protective embroidery (*oberezhnaya vyshivka*) was particularly common on linen shirts and ritual garments. Patterns such as zigzags, rhombuses, and stylized trees of life were stitched onto cuffs, collars, and hems using red thread, which itself was believed to carry protective power. These were encoded charms: the zigzag, for instance, might represent running water (a barrier to spirits) while the eight-pointed star was associated with the solar cycle and continuity of life.

In Ukrainian and Russian traditions, such embroidery was sometimes activated with speech. The person making or gifting the garment might whisper phrases as they stitched, such as "for good fate," or "may it wear well and not be cursed."

In the Nordic world, similar protective intent was embedded in textile art. Scandinavian *selburose* motifs, used in knitting and weaving, often took the form of eight-pointed stars or wheels—symbols that predate Christianity and were believed to deter evil or misfortune. In some cases, rune-like characters were embroidered into undergarments or hidden within seams, combining folk art and magical protection.

Hair-braiding, too, could be a ritual act. In Russia and Serbia, a mother might braid her daughter's hair while quietly reciting protective blessings or prayers, often beginning and ending with a cross. In parts of rural Romania and Bulgaria, a red thread or bead was sometimes woven into the braid to shield against envy. Even today, remnants of these gestures persist in the quiet instinct to "fix" a child's hair before they leave the house or to choose red accessories for good luck.

As anthropologists like E. E. Evans-Pritchard and Claude Lévi-Strauss observed, such practices are not superstitions but whole systems of symbolic logic: ways of organizing the world around threat and uncertainty. The amulet, like the spell, reflects a belief that seeks to shape outcomes and preserve what is most important.

Small Spells of Protection to Help You Through Anxiety

- Pick one object in the room and imagine it is fiercely on your side. A mug, a chair, a curtain—anything. Let it guard you in silence.

- Take a spoonful of honey and stir it into warm milk or tea while saying, "May my serenity return to me."

- Put your hand flat on your chest and hum the lowest note you can manage. Feel it echo in your ribs like a calming drumbeat.

- Draw a door on paper and write "elsewhere" above it. Tuck it in your pocket. If panic comes, you can mentally step through.

- Wet your fingertips and press them to the windowsill. Say, "I remember I am of water and sky and wind, and I will pass through this too."

- Blow on a mirror and watch the fog bloom and fade. Say, "Even this will clear."

Chapter 8

Rites of Passage

Birthdays, weddings, funerals—ancient magic hidden in life's milestones.

What if I told you that you might've participated in magic rituals even before you were born? And, even if this wasn't the case, you most certainly joined the witchy ways shortly after and have been persistently doing magic ever since, year after year?

Moments when a person transitions from one state or status to another have always been seen as both important and dangerous. The liminal, in-between nature of birthdays, weddings, and funerals was believed to both attract malevolent spirits from other realms and to open a space for useful, powerful, and benevolent magic. Ancient initiation rituals marked the shift into a new identity, helped in the crossing of one of life's thresholds, and transformed a person's essence. These rituals have been remarkably well preserved over time. The human need to "mark" a significant life passage—to give it special attention—has never disappeared.

This need was heard by newer religions, which had to offer fresh traditions but could not fully deny the old, familiar ones. Let's take a closer look at the modern lore of significant and transitional events. We'll find that much of it is ancient and magical, even if it's wrapped in customs that feel current. Is it a coincidence that baby showers resemble fairy tale christenings, where fairies arrive with gifts and blessings? Why do we sing "Happy Birthday" even when we don't particularly feel like it? Why does the bride wear a veil? And how does everyone instinctively know what to do when there's been a death in the family?

We Were All Baby Witches

Magic starts as soon as we're born…or earlier. The welcoming of a newborn is a special celebration. In ancient times, it was surrounded by layers of protective magic, and many of these rituals have been preserved to this day. Some aspects of modern customs are entirely new: for example, baby showers are now held before the baby is born, usually in the later stages of pregnancy. In the past, this would have been unthinkable: maternal and infant mortality in childbirth were too high. People often avoided even speaking openly about a pregnancy and instead kept quiet to avoid attracting misfortune. Celebrating this early was out of the question.

But aside from the shift in timing, baby showers clearly reflect ancient customs for welcoming a newborn into the world. Showering the new person with gifts and good words held great importance. Interestingly, some of these meaningful ritual gifts are still given in parts of the world today. For example, across the post-Soviet region, it is traditional to give a newborn a silver spoon (sometimes the spoon is gifted when the baby's first tooth appears). It is believed that if no one gifts such a spoon, the child will remain unprotected, and misfortune will follow them. Fairy tales in which fairies appear at a baby's christening to offer blessings and prophecies, or bestow talents, reflect this very custom: The newborn must be offered gifts and wished well, because this shapes their future.

There's a practical layer to this ancient logic that still holds true. If a baby shower brings together many guests who come bearing good gifts, support, and kind intentions, the child is clearly entering into a nurturing, favorable environment. It's a perfect example of how ancient magic can also make perfect material sense.

As soon as we are born, we get to experience another set of important and deeply magical rites: the ritual washing (and sometimes anointing with sacred oils) and the giving of a name. In modern practice, not everyone pays special attention to sacred bathing or anointing—though many people who baptize their children are, in fact, following this ancient tradition quite faithfully. The bestowing of a name, however, still feels like a significant, sacred act. In ancient times, names were very purposeful: The name might belong to an ancestor believed to have returned to the world through the newborn or it might carry a special meaning, often linking the child to protective spiritual powers or benevolent forces. The very act of naming marked a symbolic shift from the chaos of non-being to existing in the ordered world.

We may think of immersing a baby in water and giving them a name as Christian baptismal customs. But in fact, this practice is far from unique: similar rites existed in Ancient Egypt and Mesopotamia, in Japan, in the Slavic lands, and across cultures and ages. It has been a bad sign if a child was not properly welcomed into the world, not brought into it in accordance with established ritual. This belief survives even today—perhaps less strictly, but it's still very much present. The moment of birth remains the most fragile and major turning point, and we instinctively seek to protect it through rituals and customs which are always ancient at their core, but sometimes new in form.

Even your name might have been given to you in direct accordance with an ancient magical tradition! Do you know anyone who was named after their elders—most often grandparents or great-grandparents? This is still quite common: I was named after my late grandmother, and my life partner was named after his great-grandfather. Just a popular family tradition? Today, most likely, yes, but here's an interesting parallel: In archaic communities, children were usually named after deceased ancestors so that their spirit could settle in the body of the newborn. Sometimes this was done by the baby's relatives and sometimes by a shaman or priest, who was said to be able to recognize a particular deceased person in the cute little face of the child and give the new human the corresponding name.

Nowadays, some psychologists call those who were named after deceased family members "replacement children," and they note that such naming may happen not only for the sake of tradition but also from the desire to "bring back" into the family someone the parents mourn. According to this concept, being such a child is not the happiest fate, since you are seen not as your own individual person, but as a replacement for someone else. For example, a son could be named after his father who died tragically, or a younger child after an older sibling who passed away (or was never born). Psychologists point out that the line between paying tribute and transferring one's relationships and roles from the deceased onto the child can be so thin that no parent can navigate it flawlessly—so it is better to refrain from naming children after dead relatives.

Ancient people, however, believed that being a vessel for an ancestor's soul was highly beneficial, since the ancestor granted protection, strength, wisdom, support, and solid inner guidance. Such a child was treated with great respect, because they were not simply a new person—they were also a long-known and acknowledged member of the community who had returned to watch over the living.

So, the conclusions about whether such naming is desirable or not may be diametrically opposed, but the essence is similar: By giving a child the name of their deceased ancestor, we may invisibly bind their destinies together.

Dental Duet: The Tooth Mouse and the Tooth Fairy

As an example of vivid and lively children's magic, let me bring up the Tooth…Mouse. Yes, the mouse—though we'll get back to the fairy in a moment.

The best description of the roots of the tradition of offering teeth to the Tooth Mouse is found in James Frazer's *The Golden Bough*. He writes that many peoples would place a pulled or fallen tooth somewhere a rat or mouse might find it. The rat or mouse would take the tooth, and then the new tooth would sprout strong and healthy, like the powerful teeth of rodents. Frazer notes that, even in the twentieth century, German peasants sought to place pulled or fallen teeth into mouse holes—even if the tooth belonged to an adult. If it was done with a child's baby tooth, it was said that the child would be blessed with healthy teeth that never ache.

Another version of the custom was to go behind the stove and throw the tooth over one's head, saying:

> *"Mouse, give me your iron tooth.*
>
> *Here, take my bone tooth."*

The result was the same—strong teeth for life. Dentists surely would not want you to know about this!

Here is a marvelous tooth incantation from the Indigenous people of the Rarotonga island:

> *"Great Rat and Little Rat!*
>
> *Here is the old tooth,*
>
> *I beg you to give me a new one."*

And what about the Tooth Fairy? This is a fascinating case of ancient rites and beliefs that seem to vanish into the past, only to "sprout" again—though in a slightly altered form. In the thirteenth century in Northern Europe and Scandinavia, children would receive a "tand-fe" (tooth fee)—a small payment for each lost tooth. Over time, *fe* somehow evolved into *fairy*, and, by 1908, the *Chicago Tribune* mentioned the Tooth Fairy in an article. In 1927, Esther Watkins Arnold created a play of the same name.

By the way, in some countries the Tooth Mouse still reigns supreme—for example, Spain and Russia (so my milk teeth are stored in the mouse's treasury). And in Korea, this work is carried out by none other than the magpie.

I remember waiting for the Tooth Mouse almost as eagerly as I waited for my birthday. But only almost—because no matter how mysterious the mouse or the fairy might be, birthdays have their own very special kind of incomparable magic.

Birthday Sorcery

The magic doesn't stop in our infancy, of course. Every year we relive that wondrous day when we were introduced into this world. This celebration of the miracle of being born (and still hanging in there) is, of course, called a birthday.

The importance and status that birthdays hold for most people today is actually a mix of ancient and modern approaches. Throughout human history, birthdays have been celebrated, forgotten, or replaced by other commemorations. For example, Ancient Greeks and Egyptians didn't pay much attention to the anniversary of a person's birth. But the Ancient Romans did celebrate it—and their approach was in some ways quite similar to our own. *Dies natalis* was celebrated solemnly by noble Romans (while a large category of people, including women and slaves, did not have that opportunity). These celebrations included gifts, kind wishes from guests, and, of course, feasting and banquets. Round-number birthdays (jubilees) were especially lavish. Romans believed in the *genius*—a guardian spirit born with each person. This spirit was also honored and thanked on that day.

With the rise of Christianity, birthdays lost their standing in Europe. They were seen as too pagan, bordering on sorcery even, and were not encouraged by the church. But this didn't mean people were left without a yearly personal holiday: Birthdays were simply replaced by *name days*—the feast day of one's patron saint.

The Renaissance, however, became a time of rebirth, not just for the classical Greco-Roman values and aesthetic, but also for the tradition of celebrating one's birthday. Gradually, beginning with the aristocracy, birthdays—with gifts, music, guests, greetings, and special food—began to return, and by the eighteenth and nineteenth centuries, they had evolved with new traditions.

Our modern style of celebrating birthdays came about largely thanks to children's birthday parties, which became common in eighteenth-century Germany. But the tradition began in the Middle Ages—and guess what? It didn't happen without a touch of old protective magic. We have evidence of practices from the eleventh to thirteenth centuries that continued through the late medieval and early modern periods and eventually became widespread. These rituals were originally performed only for children and later came to be known as *Kinderfest*—a children's festival. As researcher Margit Grieb notes, the Germanic people believed that a child was especially vulnerable to evil spirits on their birthday, and the burning candles on the cake were meant to protect them. The candles would burn all day, and the rising smoke carried the child's wishes up to the heavens—so it was both protection and offering (for blessings and wish fulfillment).

In 1746, a massive birthday cake with candles was described at a party for Count Zinzendorf, and, in 1806, Goethe described his own cake with fifty blazing candles. In Switzerland, in 1881, the journal *Folklore* recorded the rule that a birthday cake had one candle for each year of the child's life, plus one "candle of life," and the birthday child would blow them out. These customs soon spread beyond Germany (immigrants brought them to the US and other countries).

By the twentieth century, birthdays—like many other popular holidays—became truly ubiquitous, thanks to mass media and commercialization. One might assume that, at this point, the last traces of magical meaning had vanished—but I'd argue they simply changed clothes. The candles are still there, and so is the wish. And people take that wish seriously—not just children. I'd wager most adults still take a moment to choose it carefully and secretly hope it will come true.

The importance of being surrounded by loved ones, receiving greetings, wishes, and gifts—that, too, has remained. And it's something more than just a desire to have fun. Being alone on your birthday, or not receiving any congratulations, is considered a mark of deep misfortune.

When we celebrate birthdays, we unintentionally weave together all the elements of a full, powerful ritual. Try remembering your best birthday celebrations and count how many "magic points" you earned in those moments... Here are some of the pieces of the birthday ritual:

- The cake as the centerpiece of the celebration, shared by all guests: a ritual meal that seals communal participation in the rite.
- Blowing out the candles: protective fire magic, plus invoking higher powers to grant your wish—textbook sorcery!

- Singing "Happy Birthday": a collective spell chanted together (interestingly, ancient spells were more often sung than spoken).

- Wearing festive clothes: special garments marked the moment as sacred, a way to signal to the spirits that this day deserves their attention. If the party has a dress code, consider the effect even stronger.

- Giving gifts: a classic act of protective magic, since in ancient traditions any gift was an amulet (or a hex, if given with ill intent).

- Wishing happiness, luck, health, and so on: On special days like birthdays, such words carry power, because spirits or deities are listening.

- Decorating the home or party venue: This protects the ritual space, and that protection is much needed. On your birthday, you're not just open to receiving good energy, but also more vulnerable (after all, it's a transitional, unstable liminal point in time for you).

- Those funny party hats: Believe it or not, head coverings were also thought to have protective properties.

- Celebrating milestone ages (like Sweet Sixteen, coming of age, or big jubilees): These blend birthdays with the much older tradition of life-stage initiations.

So, how many magical points have your favorite birthdays gathered?

> ## *Small Spell for Your Birthday*
>
> Save a candle from your birthday cake. Light it when you're alone, after the celebration. In its light, write a letter to yourself. Include a list of things you're proud of or genuinely happy with, including one for every year of your life. Then, find one trinket, toy, or something else that you will be pleased to see on your next birthday. This will be your present for yourself, on your next birthday. Wrap it in the letter and hide it somewhere secure. Don't forget to open your present when you're one year older.

Textbook Initiation (Literally)

Prom night feels like a party, but it has a secret. It perfectly follows the structure of ancient initiation rituals of coming of age. For many American teenagers (as well as for quite a lot of young people in other countries), it is the night when childhood slips away and a new chapter begins. The dresses, the tuxedos, the music, even the photographs—all of it works together as if it were an old ritual repeated year after year after year... And in a way, that is exactly what it is.

Anthropologists have written that rites of passage across the world often share the same pattern. First, there is separation: The young are taken out of their ordinary life. Then comes the liminal stage: the in-between time when old identities fall away and new ones have not yet settled. Finally, there is return: The community welcomes them back, but now as different people, marked by change. Van Gennep and Victor Turner observed this pattern in many cultures from Africa to Europe, and it is not hard to see the same shape in prom.

The first step is clear. On prom night, the students put aside their usual clothes. They step into something unfamiliar: gowns that make them look like royalty, tuxedos that they may never wear again. In some ways, the outfit is a signal of transformation; in older cultures, initiates wore special garments to show that they were no longer children. These clothes are almost exaggeratedly adult, serious, and not very natural for kids.

Then comes the threshold. The ballroom or gym is decorated until it barely resembles the everyday world. The lights are dim, the music takes over, and the teenagers enter a space that feels outside of time. It is liminal, in-between. Rules loosen. For one night, they are not quite children anymore but not yet fully adults. Like ancient initiations, prom night often carries a sense of both freedom and danger. Curfews are stretched, new steps are taken into romance, risks are taken. That tension belongs to the ritual itself, because this is where and when the old self is being left behind.

And then, the return. After the dance, life moves forward, but with a different tone. Graduation follows, families and neighbors begin to speak to them differently, and the young people carry a new weight. They have crossed a line, and the community sees it.

Even the smaller details echo older patterns. The crowning of a prom king and queen recalls the ancient practice of choosing symbolic rulers for a feast, figures who stand in for the whole group. The dancing itself has the feeling of festival gatherings, where music and rhythm united the community. The photographs are tokens of passage, kept like charms to remember the threshold. And the late-night parties that follow, half forbidden and half expected, recall the feasting that once came after trials of endurance.

None of this is an accident, even if it happens unconsciously. As Catherine Bell and other scholars have pointed out, ritual forms are stubborn. Even when their sacred meanings fade, their shapes endure. Prom is one of those survivors, still needed by society to tell their young, "You're no longer children."

And then, the newly crowned adults go into the world to live their adult lives... Many of them will marry at some point, and that means what? Right! More magical rituals to perform!

Marriage and Magic

Weddings are likely the most ritualized events in our modern lives. They can be carried out without any magic at all: We don't need rings, bouquets, or special garments, and we definitely don't need anything blue or borrowed to register a marriage. The fact that we often still choose to go the traditional way speaks volumes about our lingering need for powerful, proven ritual.

Marriage, at its core, is the ultimate liminal rite. As Victor Turner famously described, it's a threshold moment where two individuals step from the known world of singledom into the unknown of union, creating a new social reality. The "in-between" state of the wedding day is naturally unstable and vulnerable. It's a moment when invisible forces, both helpful and harmful, are most active. The wedding rituals we follow today have evolved precisely to navigate and protect this precarious passage.

Let's look closely at the traditions that surround weddings today and uncover their magical roots. I'll be focusing on American wedding traditions mostly, but, of course, in any country the wedding rituals are rich and spectacular.

So, we'll start with the famous rhyme many brides know by heart:

"Something old, something new,

Something borrowed, something blue,

And a silver sixpence in her shoe."

It might sound silly, but this rhyme invokes protective symbolism from the distant past. "Something old" connects the bride to her family and ancestors, anchoring her identity and strength. "Something new" holds the promise of renewal and hopeful beginnings. "Something borrowed," typically from a happily married woman, is a literal borrowing of good fortune and protective blessing. "Something blue," a color sacred since ancient times (especially in fertility rites and virginity symbolism), calls for purity, loyalty, and spiritual protection. And the "silver sixpence" was meant to secure material well-being and prosperity. Victorian England is usually credited with popularizing this rhyme, but its components are echoes of far older, cross-cultural magical traditions where layering talismans, colors, and materials warded off the evil eye and malevolent spirits during vulnerable transitions.

Next, the wedding rings—the endless circle is a universal symbol of eternity, unity, and protection. Wearing the ring on the *vena amoris* finger was believed to connect the bond directly to the heart, a magical conduit of love and life force. This symbolism persists powerfully today every time a couple exchanges rings.

The veil was once a literal shield against jealous spirits and evil forces seeking to disrupt a fragile new union. It masked the bride's identity to confuse those who might wish harm or misfortune. The act of lifting the veil represents the safe reveal and acceptance into the new communal and spiritual order.

The bouquet toss and the tradition of flower girls are rooted in fertility magic. Scattering fragrant herbs and flowers—originally not just because it looked cool, but for protection and blessing—was a way to spread good fortune among attendees. Catching the bouquet symbolized inheriting this blessing and one's readiness for the next life stage: marriage. This custom has probably stayed around so long because it is also very fun.

The wedding cake and its figurines also hold surprisingly deep meaning. The cake's tiered structure reflects the social hierarchy and layered blessings the couple enters into. Cutting and sharing cake is a communal ritual, binding families and friends into the couple's life, as if saying, "You ate cake at our wedding—now be so kind as to help us if we ever need it." And the bride/groom figurines on top of the cake surprisingly mirror ancient Slavic wedding dolls—handmade protective effigies of the couple crafted with blessings and kept in the home to guard fertility, love, and household harmony.

Bachelor and bachelorette parties—while remaining entertaining (and sometimes wild) gatherings—are also echoes of old rites of separation and preparation. In many folk traditions, including Slavic and Celtic, the days before a wedding were sacred and filled with gender-specific rituals. For brides, the "maiden's circle" was a gathering of female kin and friends who braided her hair, sang ritual songs, and passed down protective charms and advice. Songs often contained coded magic, calling on ancestral female spirits or household goddesses for protection and fertility. The ritual anointing or dressing of the bride in special garments (sometimes with hand-embroidered symbols) was another way of imbuing strength and safeguarding her liminal status. For grooms, a similar male gathering was common—a time for shared stories, tests of strength, and symbolic "last rites" of singlehood. These events served to bolster his readiness to take on marital responsibilities and ward off malevolent forces through communal solidarity. Anthropologists like Barbara Walker and Marija Gimbutas have highlighted how these gendered pre-wedding rituals were critical liminal rites, marking the end of one life stage and preparing for the next with protective magic and social integration.

Finally, the honeymoon. This term derives from ancient Europe, where "honey" symbolized sweetness and fertility and "moon" referred to the lunar cycle crucial for timing fertility and agricultural rites. The honeymoon wasn't always meant to be a vacation—it was a sacred period of time dedicated to love and, well, reproduction. In traditional communities, the newlyweds were mostly left unbothered for this time and were deemed ready to rejoin the usual work and activity right after.

Next time you find yourself at a wedding, pause and look deeper. Notice how every custom and each small detail carries echoes of magic, refined and transformed over millennia to hold safe the fragile new world two people create when they say, "I do."

Funerals and Their Solemn Sorcery

For the very end, I have left a sorrowful but inevitable part of life, one that all of us will witness sooner or later. If you have already seen someone off to the other world, you know that this process is filled with rituals and customs that are followed automatically. Grief and uncertainty feed the need for ritual: we do not know what awaits our loved ones (and one day, us) after death and the farewell ceremony must bring peace to all participants. The soul of the deceased must cross over to the other world—if it exists—and find rest there. And the relatives and friends of the deceased must begin making peace with the loss. Eventually, tranquility also has to settle.

In folk belief, these things were closely linked: The peace of the living ensured the peace of the soul in the afterlife, while, on the other hand, excessive tears and inconsolable grief could cause the deceased discomfort. For example, folklore often contains stories where the dead ask that no one cry for them anymore, because it is "salty" for them in the other world or because they are "drowning" in the tears of their relatives.

So, it is not surprising that funerals are permeated with magical rites: After all, they deal with a great mystery, one that science cannot address—the immortality of the soul and its journey after death. Of course, there are a vast number of different burial rites and traditions surrounding death. We will look at some of those traditions that are currently common in America and Europe.

A frightening picture that sooner or later comes to almost every family: a dead loved one lying in the house. One tradition we've mentioned in previous chapters connected with this moment is covering all mirrors in the house with cloth or turning them to face the wall. Why? So that the soul of the deceased does not get confused by the reflections and linger in the house. So that the spirit does not take with it the next person who appears in the mirror. So that no unclean spirits can use the mirrors as channels to enter the house—for the presence of death in the home can open such an otherworldly portal.

One should speak quietly, in a whisper, and only when necessary. Better yet, avoid conversation altogether. This seems like a natural sign of respect for the dead, and, right after a death in the family, people usually do not feel like chatting anyway. But it was also ritually important since ancient times: as I have already mentioned, death creates a portal for otherworldly spirits. Speaking may draw their attention; it is better to sit very, very quietly so that they do not come into the house or take someone from among the living.

In fact, that is exactly why people wear black to funerals and, afterwards, as mourning attire. In different countries and at different times, the color of mourning varies, but the idea behind choosing black for such circumstances is very simple: Black makes you invisible in the dark and it absorbs light. If you do not want to attract the attention of guests from the world of the dead, it is a reasonable choice. Today we are more likely to do it out of respect for the deceased and their loved ones. Black conveys the simple idea, "I am not in the mood for joy. There will be no merriment here." To come to a funeral not in black is still not only a sign of disrespect but also a kind of invitation for misfortune and trouble—few would dare risk it.

Funeral processions and the journey to the cemetery have precedent as well. In the folk traditions of many cultures, this was a necessary ritual to retrace the soul's path: to guide it from the home to its final resting place. Otherwise—as you may have guessed—the soul could linger in the house, disturbing the living and finding no peace for itself. This is why the journey with the deceased to the cemetery is so ritualized, often carefully scripted step by step. It is not merely about transporting the body; it directs the soul's attention, marking its departure from the home and its arrival at the place where it is meant to reside.

With the rise of cremation, this ritual sometimes transforms into something more prosaic: transporting the remains to the crematorium and then back home in an urn, if the ashes are not to be interred in a cemetery. Even so, many feel it is improper to leave the deceased's ashes permanently in the house. While some choose to keep the urn at home, often when the period of active mourning ends the soul is released—the ashes scattered. This is usually done in a meaningful location to the deceased: either a place they loved or wished to visit in life. Permanently keeping the ashes or refusing to scatter or bury them is often seen by relatives as an expression of excessive, all-consuming grief and an inability to let go and begin living after the loss. Something natural, but still unhealthy. And this is precisely what ancient funeral customs sought to prevent and helped avoid.

* * *

On a grave, it's essential to leave something—both permanent symbols of devotion and memory (like a headstone or cross) and small tokens of love and attention (flowers, food, keepsakes, or toys). Such offerings, and the associated communication with the dead, form an entire field of study. For now, let's briefly look at the most popular types of cemetery gifts and their magical meaning. (It's almost strange to point out the magical essence of objects whose sole purpose is to send something to the other world for the deceased… But we'll do it anyway, because not everyone considers the history behind the custom.)

The gravestone or cross is the landmark of a burial. Symbolically, it anchors and marks the spot; it shows the soul clearly that its resting place on earth is right here. Without a stone, cross, or monument, the spirit may wander restlessly. Both stone and wood were considered suitable materials for this purpose. Interestingly, wooden crosses were placed on graves even before the rise of Christianity. For example, so-called "dove crosses" in Ancient Russia were grave crosses with small, pitched roofs. They were part of Slavic pagan funeral rites, symbolizing a "house of death" for the deceased.

The fence also marked the graveyard's territory…and protected the living. Inside it, the living are guests of the dead, but, once they step outside, they return to their own space and are no longer under the power of the deceased. Leaving the fenced cemetery behind, the living do not take their dead "with them" into everyday life.

Flowers and plants are also almost obligatory gifts on graves. And it's no wonder, as vegetation has a direct connection to the underworld through its roots. Plants are literally the children of the subterranean realm where the deceased have gone. One could say that plants act as conduits for the dead...and as comfort for their loved ones, coming to honor their memory not in emptiness, but among greenery and flowers.

Traditionally, in Europe and America, the most common flowers left are roses, chrysanthemums, carnations, lilies, and irises.

Roses symbolize love, memory, and respect for the deceased. White roses are often associated with purity and spiritual peace, red ones with eternal love and deep attachment (except in China, where red flowers should not be brought to graves at all, so as not to offend the dead with such a joyful color). In pre-Christian Europe, roses were also used as protective charms, and in Roman and Egyptian graves they were laid as floral paths for the soul to help it safely pass into the other world.

Chrysanthemums are especially popular in European and Asian countries. In Germany, France, Poland, and Japan, they have long been considered flowers of memory and mourning. They symbolize immortality, rebirth, and the eternal presence of the deceased in the memories of the living.

Carnations are durable and bright, chosen for their strength and resilience. In magical logic, they protect the soul and help it find peace. In ancient Rome, carnations were used at funerals as symbols of loyalty and remembrance.

Lilies symbolize purity, innocence, and calm. In Christian tradition, they are associated with resurrection and eternal life. On ancient European and Egyptian graves, lilies also appeared as protectors guiding the soul toward the light.

Irises were used in Europe and Egypt to mark a bridge between worlds. The elongated "petals of the bridge" symbolized the path of the soul from the living to the realm of the dead.

If you want to plant something on a grave, then evergreen or coniferous plants are your best choice. They symbolize eternal life and protection. Pine and boxwood were regarded as magical plants that "close" the space, protecting the soul from evil spirits and intrusions, while also ensuring that a wandering soul or malicious force at the cemetery does not attach itself to the living.

Rosemary is another traditional option, rich with magic. Its pungent smell was associated with memory: both the ability to memorize things and the memories of our loved ones. In medieval Europe, rosemary was often planted at cemeteries. Smelling it was believed to make people remember their deceased family members, even if they were long gone.

* * *

My acquaintance, a magical practitioner, once said: "Do you know where the most expensive food is? At the cemetery. You can always find something to eat there, but you'll be paying for it for the rest of your life." People often bring food to graves, and this ritual is still regarded very seriously. To touch food meant for the dead is very likely to bring their wrath upon you or make you share their fate before your time.

In Europe and America, people often bring fruit to graves: apples, oranges, grapes. In pre-Christian Europe, apples symbolized life and immortality. Grapes represented fertility and joy; in Rome, they were placed on graves so the deceased would have nourishment in the other world.

Bread, cookies, pies, and other baked goods are more common in Eastern Europe, where they are part of the Slavic tradition. There is also a special memorial dish—*kutya*, which is essentially a sweet porridge with dried fruits.

Everywhere, candies are often left on graves. Sweets are considered especially valuable to the dead, attracting the spirit and bringing joy in the afterlife.

Drinks, too, are offered at graves (after all, the dead also need something to wash down all that candy). As early as Ancient Greek and Roman times, people poured wine or water on graves as offerings to the soul. In Mexico and Latin America, the tradition remains alive: Drinks for the dead are placed on the altar on Día de los Muertos. Bottles of vodka are not uncommon at modern cemeteries in post-Soviet countries. Along with drinks, cigarettes are often brought as well, even (interestingly) to those who never smoked in life. A common explanation you might hear is: "Well, they died—anyone might want to start smoking after such stress!" It sounds logical in its own way, but the deeper magical reasoning is somewhat different. Stimulants such as alcohol and tobacco are symbolic sources of vitality. They provide life energy and make the feeling of being alive more acute. And this is precisely what spirits, starved for vitality, lack in the world beyond.

Perhaps it would be easier just to leave money for the dead and let them buy whatever they need themselves! Of course that's a joke, and funerary beliefs don't work quite like that—but money is indeed left on graves, both in ancient times and today. The Greek custom of paying Charon for the ferry across the river Styx immediately comes to mind, but coins have been found in burials across many cultures and eras. Any item "issued" to the dead with their burial for use in the afterlife was a strong symbol that shaped their fate beyond. So money, along with weapons, jewelry, clothing, food, and so on, was a contribution to the soul's well-being. In the modern world, not everyone sees it this way, more often it is a gesture of respect. In the US, UK, Russia, and other countries, people place small coins on graves as a sign of remembrance and attention.

Candles are another obvious magical element of funerary and memorial practice. They are lit to illuminate the soul's path, to protect the living, and to help the dead in their passage beyond. The Ancient Romans and pre-Christian Europeans used fire at graves for similar purposes, believing it guarded and guided the soul. Today, candles are lit at memorial services or on personal anniversaries. The old ritual feels natural and logical, and it has been with us unbroken since ancient times in one form or another.

And then there are personal notes left at graves—sometimes confessions, sometimes words of hope that the deceased is well where they are now, and sometimes even requests for help from beyond. This is a very curious tradition, because it has its roots...in Roman necromancy! Ancient magicians brought notes with requests (or rather, commands) to the graves of criminals or unknown dead, and it was believed the spirits would carry out the requests without objection—simply because they were bored. This way, one could curse a person, cast a love spell, restore justice, punish an offender, force a thief to return money, and so on.

* * *

As you know, there is a great multitude of traditions surrounding death beyond those I have described here. It is clear that memorial feasts, days of remembrance, and other customs may also have very ancient roots and magical meaning. I have stopped at the most obvious ones—but keep digging into your culture's or family's traditions and you will find more magic.

I believe that any celebration, whether it is a birthday or a graduation, will now be more intriguing to you, since you know what magical power all these festivities contain. And even in such a sorrowful moment as saying farewell to someone, you will see a new meaning—one that offers comfort on both sides of the veil…

Chapter 9

We Are *all* Oracles

*Tea leaves, dreams, gut feelings—
how casual divination still speaks to us.*

Can the future be predicted? Even when we are sure it cannot, we often act as if it can. Perhaps there are exceptions to the rule. Or perhaps we just so deeply wish it were possible. How much easier would life be if we could get even the tiniest hint from the future?

Throughout this chapter, we'll see that the urge to know the future is an ancient, persistent human impulse. Whether through tossing a coin, reading tea leaves, observing birds, or following a fleeting hunch, we have always tried to glimpse what lies ahead. Divination lives in our games, our routines, our dreams, and even in the patterns we half-ignore in daily life. Sometimes it takes the form of careful ritual; sometimes it slips into the background, almost invisible. Yet in every case, it reminds us of a simple truth: Thanks to certain habits and practices, we are oracles ourselves.

Heads or Tails?

The canonical example of a fortune-telling method that has survived through the ages to the modern day is tossing a coin. Almost everyone has done it. It doesn't even feel like divination, because we are not trying to know the future. Often, we use this as a way to make a difficult decision. But precisely this, strangely enough, reveals both the ancient origins of such actions and their magical essence. What makes this simple way of getting a random choice between "a" or "b" so close to actual sorcery? The point is that all divination arose, long ago, from the lot.

Casting lots had a profound role: It allowed decisions to be removed from human bias and placed into the realm of the divine. Whether to begin a journey, whom to appoint as leader, what (or whom) to sacrifice, or when to plant the crops—all could be resolved by lot. In many traditions, even justice was tied to it. Disputes were settled not by argument but by letting fate decide. The methods varied, but stayed simple for a long time: tossing stones, drawing marked sticks, letting bones fall, etc.

Over time, the lot gave rise to such phenomena as games and divination. Today, they are completely separate practices, but they share a common root: the age-old human desire to hand certain decisions over to higher powers.

The Future Is an Open Book

Besides the coin, there is another old form of divination practiced even by those who had nothing to do with mysticism or spiritual service. It is called bibliomancy and is basically the act of opening a book at random and reading the passage found there as a message from higher powers. It became widespread in the Renaissance and early modern period when books became more accessible. Instructions for bibliomancy could be found, for instance, in Jewish Kabbalah and in the writings of Renaissance mystics. The Bible (or another sacred text) was often the book of choice for this practice. Allowing a book, in this random-yet-not-random way, to deliver a message from the spiritual world was not even always considered divination, so it was not something unambiguously condemned within religious tradition. It felt so natural and, at times, so enlightening that people practiced it without much hesitation or doubt.

Kids' Whimsy or Ancient Cults?

Most likely, even the most devoted skeptics tried fortune-telling in childhood. Many forms of divination have survived in modern life as part of children's games. This folklore is often reproduced for children by adults—who remember how they themselves once entertained each other this way and how much fun it was. Children also pass these practices on to other children, so the traditions spread.

There are many such ways of fortune-telling, and they are not as simple as they may seem.

Fortune-telling with a daisy promises to reveal how a certain person feels about you. You pluck the petals one by one, reciting a rhyme (or, in a simpler version, just alternating "loves me, loves me not") until the last petal remains. That final petal indicates the answer.

Where I grew up, a popular simple divination was called "rooster or hen." You hold an ear of grain by the stalk, press it between two fingers, and pull sharply upward, stripping off the tips of the seeds. If they gather evenly, it's a hen. If there are long sticking "feathers," it's a rooster. This fortune-telling reveals the gender of your future children: rooster for a boy, hen for a girl. As kids, we did it so many times that, in theory, by now we should each have dozens of children, both boys and girls...

Another popular children's divinatory game is counting crows or magpies. In different countries, there are different rhymes and signs, but the idea remains the same: The number of birds of a certain kind that you see foretells different events.

What unites all these amusements? And why do I insist that they are not so simple? In children's games, very important and fundamental predictive techniques of antiquity have survived. For example, the cults of plants and birds: The "rooster or hen" game is an echo of ancient field fertility rituals, and the counting of crows or magpies is nothing less than a simplified version of augury, the ancient Roman practice of divination through observing birds. And while adults invent new elaborate forms of fortune-telling—such as tarot or oracle cards—children have for centuries been repeating the old rituals of ancient cults...and having lots of fun in the process.

Omens and Superstitions: Blending the Old and the Modern

Superstitions intuitively seem ancient. We learned about them from our parents and grandparents, and they, in turn, most likely learned about them the same way... At the same time, some omens are not as old as they appear, which only proves their power and ability to arise whenever the time is right for them.

For example, the idea that the number thirteen foretells misfortune is rather new. It was connected with the Last Supper, since Judas the traitor was the thirteenth guest. So, the very beginning of this superstition cannot be earlier than the Christian era (so no pagan witchcraft this time). But the idea that the number thirteen, and especially Friday the 13th, foretells danger in a particularly strong way is entirely modern: It spread only in the twentieth century!

Similarly, the belief that black cats are harbingers of misfortune is not pagan but Christian in origin. It comes from the late Middle Ages and Renaissance, when black cats were linked to witches as their supposed malicious familiars. Sadly, many animal shelters today report that black cats are the least likely to be adopted. It seems people are still acting according to a superstition that clearly should have been left in the past.

In my childhood, adults often commented whenever a piece of cutlery fell on the floor. If a fork dropped, it meant a female guest was coming; if it was a knife, then our guest would be a man. Such traditions cannot be ancient either, since cutlery is a fairly recent thing along the scale of history.

There are also omens that use our own body as an oracle, and these have a higher chance of being ancient (though not always). For example, itchy palms foretell money, hiccups mean someone is thinking about you at that moment, and sneezing after certain words means confirming the truth of what was just said.

These and many other omens are things most people half-believe in. They wouldn't say they believe them, but they wouldn't ignore them. They live in the liminal zone of "maybe." Many of us keep a kind of openness and readiness for signs—we are willing to consider any message the unseen world around us might be sending.

New Times Call for New Divinations

Popular forms of divination today—tea leaves, runes, tarot and oracle cards, astrology, and many others—are, of course, not something that everyone everywhere is constantly doing. As a separate hobby (or a calling), these methods are not the focus of this book. But it is important to note just how widespread they are. People simply seem to very, very much enjoy fortune-telling—and for some, the predictions do in fact come true.

But I don't want to overlook the small and modern ways of divining. They are inobtrusive and hardly the kind of thing that builds an identity or makes someone feel like they are a powerful fortune-teller. Yet they show clearly that even those far from magic are happy to divine whenever the chance presents itself... And such a chance appears rather often, because divinatory practices are very much alive and flexible, adapting to whatever material they find in the everyday. In our time, that context is often linked to technology.

Here is just a small list of such new divinations:

- Divining by song: turning a music player or Spotify on shuffle mode and taking the first song as an answer to a question or a prediction for the day.

- Looking up a random article on Google or Wikipedia and interpreting it as a sign.

- Using a randomizer or online wheel instead of a coin toss—a digital version of heads or tails.

- Text prediction or autocorrect divination: starting a sentence and seeing what the phone writes.

- Opening Instagram or TikTok and treating the first post or ad that appears as a sign.

- Asking a question and flipping through TV channels or YouTube until you land somewhere—the result is taken as the answer.

- Looking at the license plate of the first car that passes after asking a question and interpreting its numbers and letters.

Admit it, you've done a few of these, haven't you?

And yes, of course, people rarely treat such fortune-telling with full seriousness. Yet they turn to it often, and there is always at least some degree of usefulness to these predictions.

Predicting the Future? You Must Be Dreaming!

I think even those who treat any form of fortune-telling with suspicion are not safe from participating in it. Or at the very least, we can confidently say that every single one of us practices the same art through which, throughout human history, people have received prophecies. I am speaking of dream interpretation.

We are still not sure why the brain shows us exactly these images. There are many approaches to understanding dreams, but none of them are complete. In antiquity, dreams were taken seriously as prophecies. One of the most culturally significant dreams we know was in the biblical story of the pharaoh. In his dream, he saw first seven fat cows and then seven lean ones devouring the fat cows. Priests and wise men could not explain the vision, and only Joseph, a prisoner in the dungeon, gave the correct interpretation: Egypt would see seven years of abundance and seven years of famine. This dream determined the fate of an entire nation, because, thanks to the correct interpretation, the country survived the hungry years by stockpiling food during the abundant ones.

In ancient Greece, they also knew how to listen to nightly visions. Herodotus tells us that the Athenian lawgiver Solon had a dream in which the gods warned him of a coming downfall of wealth and power. Even Alexander the Great trusted dreams: Before his campaign in Egypt, he dreamed of a gray-haired old man who showed him the way through the desert to an oasis. This route saved his army from destruction.

In ancient Rome, Julius Caesar did not heed dreams. His wife Calpurnia saw in her dream that he died in covered in blood at the foot of a statue. She begged him to postpone the meeting of the senate, but he laughed at her fear. The next day Caesar was killed by conspirators. This example went down in history as a warning that dreams should not be ignored.

A less obvious, but no less important, case comes from Mesopotamia. In the Sumerian *Epic of Gilgamesh*, the hero sees dreams before each important battle. Once he dreamed that the heavens were falling upon him, but his friend Enkidu explained that this was a sign that Gilgamesh would triumph over the monster Humbaba. In this way, the dream became a prophecy of future glory.

In Robert Moss's books on dreams and their importance in Native American culture, the wishes of the soul—which cannot otherwise emerge from the subconscious—are said to come to us in dreams. Moss writes that those hidden desires of the soul show themselves in dreams and must be carried out in life. If you dream of a party, you should have a party. Also, any good and beautiful dream must be celebrated (and recreated, if possible) in real life. Among many Indigenous tribes, Moss writes, dreams were traditionally discussed at family dinners. This way, everyone was aware of the spiritual lives of their loved ones, could guess their needs, and enjoyed time together.

In many folk traditions, dreams were not perceived in one single way: They could be a prophecy, a hidden wish, heavy thoughts seeking an outlet, or a spell cast by enemies to cloud the mind. What mattered was to pay attention to dreams and then act according to circumstances and intuition.

Even now, people still tell each other their dreams and often try to interpret them—in both psychoanalytic and prophetic ways. Popular culture (movies, TV shows, books) loves to insert prophetic dreams everywhere—this trope both hints at future events without revealing them and shows the inner world of a character. We expect something similar from dreams in real life as well.

One of the most frequent questions I get asked as a witch is, "What does this dream mean?" I believe dreams can indeed be prophetic, but this is rare. Most often, a dream is more like a message from our inner world, but our inner TV isn't always broadcasting forecasts. Much more often, it plays tangled news bulletins or fascinating series.

Go with Your Gut

No one knows how gut feelings work and what they are exactly, but everyone has one from time to time. In a way, intuition and gut feelings are much like dreams: We trust them, but not entirely. We also see them as rooted in our own psyche, yet we can't help suspecting that at times something far more mysterious is at play.

When we speak about intuition today, we usually mean a quiet, inner certainty—an answer that arrives before reasoning has time to catch up. Modern psychology has tried to explain this phenomenon in detail, and several authors have made it accessible to a wide audience.

Daniel Kahneman, in his influential book *Thinking, Fast and Slow*, describes intuition as part of what he calls "System 1" thinking. This system is fast, automatic, and often accurate, because it draws on countless past experiences stored in memory. For Kahneman, intuition is the brain's way of recognizing patterns too quickly for us to articulate. Yet he also warns that intuition can be biased and misleading, especially when it relies on stereotypes instead of real expertise.

Gary Klein offers a different perspective in *The Power of Intuition*. He spent years studying firefighters, nurses, and military commanders—people who must make split-second decisions under pressure. Klein found that experienced professionals often "just know" what to do. Their intuition is not a wild guess, but the result of knowledge built over years of practice. The brain recognizes subtle cues—like a faint change in smoke movement before a fire flashes over—and translates them into a strong feeling. In this sense, intuition can be attained, but only through deep immersion in real situations.

Another well-known exploration is Malcolm Gladwell's *Blink*. Gladwell focuses on the power of first impressions, showing how snap judgments sometimes outperform deliberate analysis. He describes art experts who instantly recognize a forgery or tennis coaches who predict a double fault before the racket touches the ball. His main point is that thin slices of information, if processed by an experienced mind, can yield remarkable insights. However, like Kahneman, he acknowledges the danger of relying on intuition without awareness of its limits.

Another idea comes from Gerd Gigerenzer in *Gut Feelings: The Intelligence of the Unconscious*. He argues that intuition is not irrational at all—it is a form of "fast and frugal" reasoning that helps us navigate a complex world. According to Gigerenzer, simple rules of thumb, guided by gut feelings, can often lead to better outcomes than sophisticated calculations. For example, when choosing investments, trusting a basic recognition heuristic can sometimes outperform expert financial models.

Together, these books suggest that intuition is both ancient and practical: It emerges from unconscious pattern recognition, can be sharpened through practice, and often deserves trust—though not blind obedience.

* * *

This modern understanding resonates with older, mythic stories. In ancient cultures, ignoring inner warnings was often equated with defying the gods. A famous example comes from the tragic figure of Cassandra in Greek mythology. Gifted by Apollo with the ability to glimpse into the future, she foresaw the fall of Troy and begged her people not to bring the wooden horse within the city walls. Yet her curse was that no one would believe her. The Trojans dismissed her warnings as madness, and, by ignoring her prophecy, they sealed their destruction. The lesson here is clear: A truth that cannot be rationally explained may still hold the power of survival.

Another case appears in Homer's *Odyssey*. Odysseus receives repeated warnings not to let his crew slaughter the sacred cattle of Helios, the sun god. Both the prophet Tiresias in the underworld and the enchantress Circe caution him. Yet when hunger overcame the sailors, they ignored the divine prohibition and killed the animals. The punishment was swift: Zeus sent down a storm that wrecked their ship, leaving Odysseus as the sole survivor. Here again, the refusal to heed an inexplicable but insistent warning—"Don't touch what isn't yours"—led to catastrophe. Ancient audiences would have understood this as a lesson in trusting the gods' will, even when it conflicted with immediate logic or need.

Roman historians also preserved this idea in detail. Livy, in his *History of Rome*, recounts multiple episodes where generals ignored omens to their peril. One striking example is the case of Consul Claudius Pulcher during the First Punic War. Before a naval battle in 249 BCE, he ordered sacred chickens to be released for augury, a ritual meant to determine divine favor. When the birds refused to eat—a clear sign of bad fortune—he mocked the ritual and threw them into the sea, saying, "If they will not eat, let them drink!" He then attacked anyway and suffered a crushing defeat at Drepana. For the Romans, this was not just military miscalculation but arrogance against the gods, and Claudius was recalled in disgrace.

Even outside grand wars, the principle repeated itself: a sign, however strange, was to be respected. In Livy's narrative, generals who paused or changed plans because of unusual omens often fared better than those who pressed forward in defiance. To ignore the signs was seen not as bravery but as hubris, a dangerous belief that human logic alone could outweigh divine intelligence.

* * *

If we look closer, the mechanism is not so different from what psychologists describe today. Ancient people called it the will of the gods; we might call it the unconscious processing of information. In both cases, something larger than deliberate reasoning gives direction. The decision to follow or ignore it makes the difference.

For example, Klein's firefighters act on gut feelings that save lives. They may not be able to explain why they rushed out of a building seconds before it collapsed, but their bodies had already registered subtle cues, like heat, sound, and air pressure. To them, it feels like a warning from nowhere like an omen. Ancient people would have said a god pulled them by the sleeve.

At the same time, Kahneman's warning against biases mirrors the caution in old stories. Myths are full of false prophets and misleading visions. The Greeks knew that not every oracle was to be trusted; sometimes the gods themselves deceived mortals. Similarly, today we know intuition can misfire, producing overconfidence or prejudice. Discernment remains essential.

So how can intuition be trained? Klein suggests practice in realistic settings—decision games, simulations, and after-action reviews. Gigerenzer recommends embracing heuristics instead of suppressing them and paying attention to bodily signals and gut reactions. Kahneman advises humility: test your intuitions against evidence. In practice, this means listening to the inner voice, but verifying its directions when the stakes are high.

If we put it all together, intuition becomes both a modern psychological tool and an echo of ancient wisdom. Our ancestors treated sudden certainties as messages from gods; today we see them as the unconscious intelligence of the brain. The core advice remains unchanged: Do not dismiss the quiet inner nudge. It may be pointing the way to survival, insight, or success—even if the reason is hidden from view and seems highly mysterious.

I think all of this together suggests that most of us are, in a way, "spontaneous oracles." We divine whenever the moment arises—sometimes taking to heart a horoscope that appeared by chance in our feed, sometimes avoiding a bad sign, sometimes pondering a dream in search of a clue, sometimes acting on intuition even if it seems far from logical. Divinatory practices have woven themselves into our everyday lives: so naturally and in such small ways that we glance toward the future only out of the corner of the eye—yet we do so often.

Small Spell: Bibliomancy

Here's a powerful, yet casual way of divination: Open a book to a random page (or a page chosen by a specific magical algorithm). I know you've got at least one book, so everything you need is already at hand.

Here are several ways to ask a book for guidance:

- On the random page you open to, read the first paragraph your eyes land on. Try to interpret this text as an answer to your question, or, if you didn't ask a specific question, simply as a message or hint meant just for you. Read between the lines: The meaning of such messages isn't always literal, so engage your imagination and try to see metaphors that apply to your life or feelings.

- Check how many pages your book has. Choose a number within that range. Then pick a second number to determine the line. You can ask a question or just look for a general message. Find the page corresponding to your first number, and count lines from the top until you reach the second number. If you continue onto the next page, that's fine—the important thing is to reach the line with the chosen number. That line is your answer.

- Formulate your question briefly and clearly. Write it down, then convert it into numbers: each letter becomes a number according to its place in the alphabet (for example, A = 1, Z = 26). Add up all the numbers. Their sum is the page in the book where you should look for your answer. If the sum is larger than the number of total pages, add the digits together (for example, 4,444 = 4+4+4+4 = 16), so your page number is sixteen.

- If you have many books and don't know which one to assign a prophetic role to this time, you can, for example, open the third book on the shelf with a blue cover. The number and color can be chosen randomly, or you can match them to your question or current situation. For example, if the question is about love, you might pick the second red-covered book, because two is a couple, and red symbolizes romance.

- Don't consult the book whenever you feel like it, but when the book wants to tell you something. If a book falls on the floor or suddenly appears somewhere you didn't expect it, or you encounter a mention of a certain book you have three times during the day, this book, right now, has a message for you. It's best to consult it.

- Here's also a method that works for ebooks: Flip through the book on the screen with your eyes closed, mentally asking your question. The page you stop on when your question is fully asked is where your answer is.

Chapter 10

Momentary Magic

Blowing out candles, making wishes, noticing lucky numbers: tiny acts, timeless power.

Much of what was described in the previous chapters can be called tradition or everyday customs with forgotten ancient roots. But now we'll turn to pure magic, which absolutely every one of us has practiced at some point in life.

After all, what is magic? At its core, it's the expression of your will ("I want this to happen!") plus certain actions or special circumstances considered magical. And, perhaps most importantly, the belief that some higher forces will now take your wish into their care. All three boxes are checked when we make wishes. Some people do this rarely—maybe once or twice a year, on their birthday and on New Year's Eve. Others use every convenient chance to ask anonymous, unseen powers for a small piece of luck.

In this chapter, we'll uncover how simple actions—blowing out candles, noticing patterns in nature or numbers, tossing a coin into water—are actually very old ways to influence fate itself! You'll see that these tiny acts carry surprising depth: Some are inherited from centuries-old magical traditions, while others have emerged more recently and were shaped by modern life and technology. By paying attention to these moments, you can recognize the subtle ways magic might help your wishes actually come true, or you might just learn to participate in it knowingly, making everyday life feel a little more enchanted.

Let's take a closer look at the most popular scenarios for making wishes and attracting good fortune. And let's figure out which ones are directly descended from ancient magic, and which ones are fairly new.

Magic for Kids (That They Take to Adulthood with Them)

The first wish-making spells that we learn are easy, funny, engaging, and known to us since early childhood. They are often connected to commonplace, easy-to-miss things.

Of course, the birthday cake. We've already talked about candles in this book more than once—both in and out of the context of birthdays—so there's no need to repeat it again. What matters for this chapter is that, in most cases, this is the very first act of wish-making we learned as children.

Try to remember, if you can, how adults explained this yearly ritual to you. Or maybe you recall how, once you were grown, you told a child to blow out the candles and make a wish. Did it seem to you that the answers to questions like "Why?" and "Will it really come true?" were so obvious they didn't need words? Have you noticed that if you actually try to answer and explain this ritual it turns out to be trickier than you'd think?

Everyone's experience will be different here, but I think this example shows well the fascinating, elusive, and double-sided nature of wish-making. It's simple and natural...and at the same time wrapped in mystery. We know why we do it—but do we really? We expect the wish to come true—but don't actually understand why or how it should happen. We rarely stop to reflect on things like this. Maybe that's for the best: The irrationality of magic doesn't split neatly into "fact" and "superstition." When those ingredients are mixed together into that familiar enchanted soup, the magic works better (and soup is good for you).

There are other popular rituals for making wishes—and we're often "trained" in them from early childhood. For example, if you're standing or sitting between two people with the same name, you should make a wish. (For me and my peers, this was very popular since kindergarten—parents, teachers, and even the children themselves would remind you to do this in case you forgot.)

If an eyelash falls out, you're supposed to place it on the tip of your finger and blow it away while making a wish. People constantly remind each other about this too, especially young kids. "You've got an eyelash, let me get it!" one child tells another, carefully moving the fallen eyelash from their friend's cheek onto their own finger, then holding it up so the eyelash's owner can blow it away and silently wish for what they most desire. This little friendly ritual builds trust between children—it's a kind of magical mutual aid, since a good friend is expected not to keep silent about an eyelash and to help their friend not miss their chance to make a wish.

And there are more magic rituals tied to our bodies. As I've mentioned before, it's said that if you sneeze once, it confirms whatever was just said: Those words are now presumed to be true. But if you sneeze three (or four) times, then you can make a wish. This idea, by the way, is quite ancient. People didn't always understand how sneezing works physiologically. It seemed obvious that spirits or some otherworldly forces had a hand in it—that it was their way of showing themselves through our body.

Wishing Wells: Bless or Curse Anyone for a Small Donation

When I first went to the Black Sea with my mother, on the last day of our trip she gave me a coin and said, "Throw it into the sea, so that you'll come back here again." I threw the coin, and the act felt solemn and serious. It seemed that my return was now settled…as I had already paid for it.

I never returned to that exact beach, and most likely I never will. But I have been back to the Black Sea several times since, and later to other breathtakingly beautiful seas, lakes, and rivers. And every one I went to, I threw a coin into the water (truth be told, I even tossed quite a few into city fountains, if I happened to like them). This tradition has always felt perfectly logical and clear to me, even though it never comes with any explanations. Everyone says you can toss a coin to ensure your return, but no one follows it up with something like, "The spirits of this fountain will hear your request and bend the lines of your fate so that you end up here again." Countless people do it, and very few have a consistent theory about what mechanism lies behind it. The way we perceive magic often works just like that—without requiring explanations. Still, the example of a coin in the water is a striking one: We expect a fairly high level of effectiveness from the ritual, even when we don't believe in spirits, fate, or gods.

The tradition I described coexists with another one which is most likely much older. In different corners of the world, so-called wishing wells still exist.

It is often said that the tradition of throwing coins into wells to make wishes originated in medieval Europe. But if you dig deeper (pun intended), it becomes clear that this tradition resurfaced and was reinvented in the Middle Ages. In fact, offerings to water spirits and showing reverence to springs existed throughout all known human history and, most likely, beyond.

Wishing wells became an iconic image in video games and, of course, they still exist in real life. Some of them do look quite "medieval," like in fantasy games. But most of the best-known and most visited ones today are, technically, more like fountains—for example, the Frankfurt Wishing Wells, the Trevi Fountain in Rome, or the Fountains of Peterhof in St. Petersburg, Russia. Such places are often associated exclusively with tourism, and locals look at the crowds of foreigners showering the landmarks with coins with a smile...or even with disapproval. But not only tourists are inclined toward mysticism. Sacred, revered, even magical springs and bodies of water are found in most local communities, though the traditions connected with them rarely leak into the public media. For example, quite often water cults that survived into modern times flowed into the dominant religious tradition. Christian monasteries often have their own "holy spring," the water from which is considered blessed by God or saints and believed to carry special, miraculous properties. Throwing coins into them is generally not encouraged, but offerings are still required. For example, many monasteries offer candles for purchase in chapels or have special donation boxes for the needs of the monastery.

And, as I mentioned in Chapter 1, wishes to magical wells were not exclusively kind and bright. In some regions, a coin or some other offering to the spirits of sacred wells and springs guaranteed a deal with unclean forces, which could benefit the giver or cast harm on their enemies. And such practices were popular not so long ago—for example, it was still popular in the Russian Empire at the beginning of the twentieth century!

Naturally Lucky

All is well that's found in nature—even if it's not a well. Nature is the richest source of luck and opportunities for wish fulfillment. For example, it was in nature that one had to look for strong talismans (objects attracting luck) and amulets (objects blocking evil). This could be a stone with a round hole in the middle (in some places these are called "chicken gods," because they were hung in henhouses to protect the birds). It could also be a so-called fairy rock—a stone with stripes that encircle it completely without a break in the pattern. They say if you run your finger along this line, you'll attract luck. Unusual feathers, sticks, bones, or even animal remains could also be especially valued objects attracting luck. If a natural object was unusual—this meant it was marked by spirits or gods and therefore endowed with power. If it came from an animal—it carried within itself the magical properties and protection of that animal.

Perhaps nowadays we've shifted toward talismans and amulets that have personal meaning for us—from wedding rings to certain thrifted trinkets dear to our hearts. However, there's this special feeling when you walk in nature: You want to pick up and examine unusual pebbles, branches, acorns, feathers... And if one of them somehow seems to look right into your soul and says, "I'm here especially for you!" we take it home. We may not know exactly why, and we usually don't expect anything from our finds, but we treat them as magical objects of sorts.

Nature is full of wish-making opportunities. When you see the first butterfly of the year. When you catch a dandelion or poplar fluff (let it fly to carry your wish to the sky). When you find a five-petaled lilac flower (eat it or put it under your pillow for your wish to come true). When you find a four-leaf clover (carry it with you). When you see a falling star or a double rainbow... You don't even need to believe in magic to do this. The magic of such things is so simple and natural that it happens to everyone who takes a bit of time to make their wish. This practice is much more about living an enchanted life than about the wishes being always promptly fulfilled.

Angel Numbers: Fake or Real?

Many people nowadays make wishes when they notice repeating numbers on clocks—for example, 11:11 or 4:44. Spotting a car license plate or any other sign with these numbers is also a reason to send a request to the universe and feel lucky. Some people have heard that such numbers hold a certain kind of magic. Others know that these are called Angel numbers, and that each set of numbers has its own meaning. It's a special method by which angels—or the universe—reach out to us. Only those who are more deeply immersed in esotericism know the origin story (and some even feel somewhat skeptical about the whole topic).

The idea of Angel numbers was introduced by Doreen Virtue, a former famous esoteric author who rejected it all in 2017 and claimed to no longer practice anything esoteric. For some people, this puts great doubt on everything she did before, including the Angel numbers concept.

But the question is: Was it all made up from scratch or taken from somewhere?

As we examine everything carefully, we can see that the idea of the divine world communicating with us through numbers is far from new. Angel numbers weren't, strictly speaking, invented by anyone. They were reintroduced to the modern world and given a fresh, digestible form and a catchy title (which is really great!). Numerology, the symbolic and magical meaning of numbers, is a concept known since ancient times to Greeks, Egyptians, and Romans. The idea of angels giving us messages and signs isn't that new either.

What *is* new is our digitized world, where we see numbers more often than, say, the people in ancient Greece. Our screens are projecting loads of numbers all the time, and that's exactly why we often can't see a sign in a single number anymore. Instead, we need to pay attention to their combinations and sequences. That's why the idea of seeing 11:11 on your screen and reading it as a message is relatively new. What's not new is the symbolism of the individual numbers and the whole concept of angels, or other spirits, sending us their messages and guidance in the form of numbers. So, no, Angel numbers aren't fake. At least, they were taken very seriously in one form or another since the ancient period.

In fact, the idea that numbers bring luck or allow you to make a wish is actively and continuously shaped in the modern world, independent of Angel numbers or the popularity of numerology. These ideas emerge with new scenarios where we encounter sequences of numbers and fade away when those scenarios pass.

For example, during my childhood, bus, trolley, and tram tickets in Russia each had a six-digit number. Everyone, children and adults alike, knew that when you got a ticket, you had to look at the numbers. If the sum of the first three digits equaled the sum of the last three, it was a "lucky ticket." You were supposed to make a wish and, to have it come true, either eat the ticket or place it under your pillow. But somewhere around 2010, these tickets began to disappear, replaced by transit passes of a different type that no longer carried the six-digit code. Lucky tickets once were known all over the country to everyone, and then, with the next wave of technological change, they quietly vanished from the scene.

This shows that numbers have their own kind of magic—at least in our minds. We don't just preserve ancient ideas about them; we actively invent new ways to read them and new little spells to activate their powers. Nowadays, someone might comment under my social media post: "My like is number 444, I'm claiming this positive energy!" And if likes themselves someday vanish into the dustbin of history, I'm sure we, as humans, will find another way to find divine numerical messages.

Personal Lore

Do you have your own special traditions that call for making a wish at a certain moment? Or perhaps you recall a family member or friend saying that they see a certain event as especially lucky for them? Almost all of us have these personal lucky signs—even if we don't always remember them. Often, these signs are tied to the environment we live in; for example, someone might make a wish while walking under a bridge that happens to have a train passing over it at that exact moment. Another person might see the turning on or off of city lights as a sign that a dream is about to come true. For someone else, a chance encounter with a favorite bird brings good news, or a wish is made when eating a unique, "double" strawberry.

We're eager to call certain situations or coincidences lucky, and usually it doesn't take much confirmation. Maybe someone once told us that a wish could be made at a particular moment. Maybe it's part of a traditional tourist ritual—like tossing a coin into a fountain or touching a specific sculpture "for good luck." Maybe the sign is connected to a beloved person who believed in it. Or maybe it's tied to a happy moment from our past.

Making a wish is an intuitively understandable process, and skepticism about it is much lower than, say, with divination or elaborate witchcraft rituals. I think this process actively engages our "inner child," as well as all our memories of fairy tales and folk beliefs. In the end, even a completely serious person, one who doesn't believe in anything paranormal, will blow out the candles on a birthday cake or tell their child, "Look, a shooting star! Quick, make a wish."

At the end of the day, the magic of wishes isn't about elaborate rituals or guaranteed results. It's about noticing the small, fleeting moments when the world seems to pause, giving us a chance to express our desires and hopes. Some of these practices connect us to ancient traditions, while others are born from our own imagination—but all of them remind us that life has its own kind of enchantment. By paying attention, by participating even in the tiniest ways, we keep that wonder alive, and we make space for a little bit of the extraordinary in our ordinary days. Magic, it turns out, is less about bending the universe and more about opening ourselves to its possibilities and expressing our hopes, strong and fragile at the same time.

Small Spell to Make Wishes More Often

Write down everything you wish for, each wish on a separate piece of paper. Roll all the papers up into little scrolls. Put them all in a small bag or a special little purse and take them with you everywhere in your handbag or backpack.

Every time something from the upcoming Wishmaking List happens, pick one scroll at random, open it, read your wish, feeling confident that it will come true for you when the time is right. After that, smile and put the scroll back in the bag. You may pull it again and again, if the fates decide so. Remove a scroll from the bag only when that wish has come true!

You can add new wishes anytime. (In fact, it would be great if you do!)

The Wishmaking List
(You Can Add to It, Too, If You Want)

- When you blow out your birthday candles
- When you're standing or sitting between two people with the same name
- When you see the first butterfly of the year
- When you lose an eyelash (you need to blow it from your finger)
- When you see repeating numbers on the clock
- When you catch dandelion or poplar fluff (let it fly to carry your wish to the sky)
- When you get a ticket with an even digit number (for example, six digits), and the first half of the digits add up the same as the second half (for example, 111 102)
- When you find a five-petaled lilac flower
- When you find a four-leaf clover
- When you see a falling star
- When you sneeze three or four times in a row
- When you walk under a bridge right when a train is crossing it
- When you catch the moment when streetlights come on or go out

- When you see a double rainbow

- When you toss a coin into water (a well, a pool, a pond, a stream, the sea, etc.)

- When you find a heads-up penny

- When you see your favorite animal or bird three times or more in one day

- When you hear someone calling your name, but it's not you they're addressing

- When you blow all the fluff from a dandelion with one blow

- When you precisely predict in your mind the next phrase said by someone

Conclusion

Living a Life Lit with Magic—Whether You Believe or Not

Well, dear readers, do you feel like real witches now? In truth, that doesn't matter all that much.

If the themes of witchcraft and magic don't particularly resonate with you, then another no less important—and perhaps even more universal—thing may come to the forefront: a living connection to the past. Many modern people feel cut off from history, locked inside their own era. This is confirmed both by social anthropologists and the enormous amount of content on social media that tries in some way to bridge this gap, like memes about being born in the wrong time, posts with slides of "your medieval castle," or thousands of comments under photographs of historical artifacts (many of which read like "desperately need this in my life"). Many of us long for times we never lived in and feel absolutely disconnected from the meaningful and sacred. Ordinary, modern life seems like a bleak drag.

But what I have described in this book is meant to show the bright historical roots of familiar things that once had immense meaning in antiquity and were taken with utter seriousness. Modernity often seems banal—even its festive moments, such as the winter holidays, are often perceived as vulgar, stripped of meaning, and hidden beneath layers of commercialization. But if we call upon knowledge of their true nature—magical, ritualistic, and existentially essential to ancient people—we help them regain their power. And with that, our own lives become filled with profound, historical, and valuable practices, objects, and traditions...even if we haven't actually changed a single thing about them!

Magic and faith are vital parts of the history of any society. They make people of every era more alive, giving them meaning, hope, stories, and shared experience. They continue to do this for us even now—and I hope that my book has shown you where to look in order to notice and feel it for yourself.

* * *

Or perhaps, on the contrary, you must have anything with "witch" written on it? If so, I understand you very well—I'm exactly the same. From early childhood, my attention was unwaveringly captivated by any mention of magic. I don't know why exactly, but I felt that if true meaning existed anywhere, it was in magical things. (On the other hand, if I happened to like something, say rocks or frogs, then surely they must be endowed with magic in some way.)

For those who are already connected with magical practices in one way or another, it can be helpful to see that truly simple objects—or traditions that seem entirely secular (or even vaguely religious)—can also be magical. Complex rituals with exotic ingredients are wonderful, but I know that many practicing witches feel guilty or "not real" enough because they can't perform such rites all the time. Often, there's not enough energy, time, money, or even focus to "properly" carry out a ritual—but that doesn't mean we are less worthy or authentic! Practice your craft, study, and keep discovering new facets of magic, but don't forget that wonders are already happening all around you. These are not empty words; such wonders were seen and acknowledged by ancient people, the very ones who left us a legacy of myths, magical practices, and ideas about the spiritual world. When you know that a cup of milk with a round bun carries important magical meanings and deep ritual history, it becomes easier to remain awestruck. The magical "nourishment" we need for our energy comes quite literally from the surrounding world.

* * *

Still, I doubt I'd be wrong to assume that most readers will find themselves somewhere in-between: The magical is not foreign to you, but you would hardly call yourself a witch. Magic has value and draws you in. You look for it in books and fantastic worlds, but you are not sure whether you believe in its power.

You are very lucky; you have already discovered how interesting life can be when you look at it through a prism of wonder. Once, I posted on my social media, "I don't romanticize. I sacralize." It became very popular, and I understand why: to romanticize life is a huge, deep need for many people. But romanticization is usually about aesthetics and partly about emotions. Naturally, one wants to go further—and include a deep sense of meaning in the process. That is why the idea of sacralization instead of romanticization resonated so strongly with people. And that is why we want so deeply to find magic in our lives and keep it as close as possible to our everyday routines.

But here comes the big question: What practical steps can we take to find this magic in our lives and history? Well, one of these steps, I hope, has been this book. But don't stop here.

Start with your family—ask your relatives about traditions and beliefs that are important and meaningful to them. Questions that are too general can leave a person at a loss ("Where is magic in your life?"), since we usually don't think about such things. Be more specific. "Have you ever experienced any supernatural or unexplained events?" "What was considered a bad omen in your family? And what was considered a good one?" "How did you and your parents celebrate the winter holidays?" "On which days did your older relatives usually visit the graves of family members? What did they do there?" "If you wanted to tell your fortune or have a psychic experience, what would you do? Who would you turn to? How did that usually work?"

Some information can only be received by listening carefully and being attuned to the unusual and the magical, so stay open to what older generations talk about. You can easily encounter living, uncontrived magic there.

Notice also the modern rituals you come across. What brings luck to your friends? In what way do you use the internet for spells? (Yes, that "special" Pinterest board counts, too!) What things act as talismans and significant artifacts, even if they were mass-produced in the thousands? And which of the pieces of knowledge that we use are actually very ancient? (For example, right now I am drinking chamomile tea to calm my nerves and stomach. I feel a pleasant magical aftertaste from knowing that chamomile has been used in the same way by many generations of wise people who considered it a wondrous plant.)

Keep looking for books that help your manifestation of wonder stay clear and strong. In bookstores, magic lives not only on the shelves with fantasy novels or modern witchcraft spellbooks, but also in anthropology, culture, and history sections. And I always find the rarest and most valuable works when I take the time to see what is being published by nearby institutes or colleges specializing in anthropology, folklore studies, art history, and related disciplines. What you can find there is worth the trip to these institutions and the careful search through their bookshops, which often sell their publications. Often, this is almost the only way to study local culture with its traditions, folklore, and magic through books.

And, in general, the place you live is almost certainly filled with magic. Of course, it is not immediately obvious, but try to look around you like you're a paranormal investigator. Notice what celebrations and festivities the locals hold and what rituals are part of them. Explore the history of your region—as far back into the past as you can trace it. Find out if there are legends or conspiracy theories connected with the area. Which sites are considered haunted or creepy, and which, on the contrary, are visited for luck? Perhaps you want to explore a cemetery or some other place connected with the otherworld. One way or another, if you compile a magical dossier on your corner of the Earth, you will discover an incredible amount of mystical things in the process.

* * *

There is a well-documented thread in European folklore about magical ointments—sometimes called "fairy ointments"—that grant the ability to see the hidden world of the fairies or spirits.

This theme is especially strong in Celtic and British folklore. A common story goes like this: A midwife is called to attend a fairy birth. She is instructed not to touch her eyes with the ointment she is given to anoint the newborn. Out of curiosity, she touches one eyelid, and suddenly she can see the fairies in their true form and perceive their invisible world interwoven with ours.

When I read these stories as a child, I was sad that I didn't have this ointment: I wanted to see the world of the fairies with my own eyes so much! Lacking this concoction, I searched for anything that could help me see that magical world, though in a more complicated way. The study of the little acts of magic that permeate everyday life became my way of seeing the fairy world. I hope this book, the result of years of study, magic, and wonder, can become a drop of fairy ointment for you and opens your eyes to the magic all around us.

Further Reading

Bodel, John. "Cicero's Minerva, *Penates*, and the Mother of the *Lares*: An Outline of Roman Domestic Religion." In *Household and Family Religion in Antiquity*. Wiley-Blackwell, 2012.

Bouattou, Bachir. *The Symbolism of Animals in Different Traditions: Anthropological Viewpoint*. Our Knowledge Publishing, 2023.

Carr-Gomm, Philip, and Richard Heygate. *The Book of English Magic*. Hachette, 2010.

Eliade, Mircea. *Patterns in Comparative Religion*. Bison Books, 1996.

Gimbutas, Marija. *Ancient Symbolism in Lithuanian Folk Art*. American Folklore Society, 1958.

Gimbutas, Marija. *The Language of the Goddess: Unearthing the Hidden Symbols of Western Civilization*. Harper, 1991.

Gimbutas, Marija. *The Slavs*. Praeger, 1971.

Grimassi, Raven. *Italian Witchcraft: The Old Religion of Southern Europe*. Llewellyn Publications, 2000.

Hole, Christina. *A Dictionary of British Folk Customs*. Paladin, 1978.

Jackson, Jake, ed. *Slavic Myths*. Flame Tree 451, 2023.

Lehner, Ernst, and Johanna Lehner. *Folklore and Symbolism of Flowers, Plants and Trees*. Dover Publications, 2003.

Leland, Charles Godfrey. *Stregheria*. Self-published, 2017.

Malinowski, Bronislaw. *Magic, Science and Religion and Other Essays*. Beacon Press, 1948.

McLaren, Angus. *Reproductive Rituals: The Perception of Fertility in England from the Sixteenth Century to the Nineteenth Century*. Routledge, 1984.

Propp, Vladimir. *Morphology of the Folktale*. American Folklore Society, 1968.

Santino, Jack, ed. *Halloween and Other Festivals of Death and Life*. University of Tennessee Press, 1994.

Turner, Victor. *The Ritual Process: Structure and Anti-Structure*. Cornell University Press, 1969.

van Gennep, Arnold. *The Rites of Passage*. University of Chicago Press, 1960.

Wrangham, Richard. *Catching Fire: How Cooking Made Us Human*. Profile Books, 2009.

Acknowledgments

My heartfelt gratitude goes to the entire Key Lime Publishing team for believing in me and in this idea from the very beginning.

To my editor, Hugo Villabona, thank you for guiding me along this journey with such care and attention and for helping this book become something far better than my words could have shaped alone.

To my magical beings—my readers and followers—this book would not have come to life without you. For four years you have been my constant inspiration, and, in the darkest moments, the thought of more than 400,000 kindred spirits out there who share my love of all things strange and wondrous has kept me going.

To my soulmate, Khvost—my family, my teammate, my fellow forest hedgehog on cozy quests—thank you for everything.

To my mom, Ian, and to Lipa, for simply being so wonderful.

And to the city of Belgrade, where books seem to write themselves.

About the Author

Lida Pavlova is a writer, tarot creator, and magical practitioner whose work bridges mysticism and creative exploration. Her journey began in 2011 with professional tarot reading and magical practices which evolved into a multifaceted creative path that includes writing, deck design, and folklore research.

Her first book was published in Russian in 2014. In summer 2025, she published her debut book in English *The Library of Questions: Unconventional Tarot Spreads and Journaling Prompts*, an extensive self-published guide to deepening intuitive and creative practice through tarot and journaling.

Lida has created and published four tarot decks—*Honey and Lavender Tarot*, *PHRÖG TAROT*, *Bird King Tarot*, and *The Green Tarot*—as well as the *Ominous Oracle* deck.

Between 2013 and 2022, her work was widely featured in major Russian media. Now based in Serbia, she continues to expand her international presence, including a recent in-depth interview in *Plezir Magazine*, published in both Serbian and English.

Lida's work is known for its poetic vision, symbolic depth, and ability to spark personal transformation. Whether through cards or words, she invites her audience into a richer dialogue with intuition and the unknown.

Key Lime Publishing is an independent publisher founded by former members of the award-winning Mango Publishing team. Collectively, we've published more than 1,000 books since 2014, selling over 10 million copies and earning national recognition along the way. Now, we're channeling that experience into reimagining what publishing can be in a rapidly changing world.

Our mission is simple yet ambitious: to empower new and underrepresented authors, connecting their voices with readers in authentic, meaningful ways, while staying agile in the face of the challenges reshaping the publishing industry. From the rise of AI to shifting global supply chains, inflationary pressures, and industry uncertainty, the landscape of 2026 and beyond demands resilience, creativity, and bold new strategies.

That's why Key Lime is harnessing the experience of building one of fastest-growing independent publishers in the US over the last decade to create a publishing house tailored to modern authors looking to connect with their audience and new readers.

Please stay in touch with us and follow us on our website (keylimepublishing.com) and Instagram (@KeyLimePublishing).

Thanks for reading!

www.ingramcontent.com/pod-product-compliance
Lightning Source LLC
Chambersburg PA
CBHW011549070526
44585CB00023B/2521